Home Schooling and Home Education

Home Schooling and Home Education provides an original account of home education and examines ways in which the discourses of home education are understood and contextualised in different countries, such as the UK and the United States. By exploring home education in the global and local context of traditional schooling, the book bridges a much-needed gap in educational and social scientific research.

The authors explore home education from two related perspectives: firstly how and why home education is accessed by different social groups; and secondly, how these groups are perceived as home educators. The book draws upon empirical case study research with those who use home education to address issues of inequality, difference and inclusion, before offering suggestions for viable policy shifts in this area, as well as broadening understandings of risk and marginality. It engages and initiates debates about alternatives to the standard schooling model within a critical sociological context.

The scholarly emphasis and original nature of *Home Schooling and Home Education* makes this essential reading for academics and postgraduate researchers in the fields of education and sociology, as well as for educational policymakers.

Kalwant Bhopal is Professor of Education and Social Justice at the University of Birmingham.

Martin Myers is Lecturer in Education Studies at the University of Portsmouth.

Routledge Research in International and Comparative Education

This is a series that offers a global platform to engage scholars in continuous academic debate on key challenges and the latest thinking on issues in the fast-growing field of International and Comparative Education.

Titles in the series include:

Home Schooling and Home Education
Race, Class and Inequality
Kalwant Bhopal and Martin Myers

Politics of Quality in Education
A Comparative Study of Brazil, China and Russia
Edited by Jaakko Kauko, Risto Rinne and Tuomas

China's Global Rise
Higher Education, Diplomacy and Identity
Su-Yan Pan

Educational Choices, Aspirations and Transitions in Europe
Systemic, Institutional and Subjective Constraints
Edited by Aina Tarabini and Nicola Ingram

Cooperative Education in Asia
History, Present and Future Issues
Edited by Yasushi Tanaka

Testing and Inclusive Schooling
International Challenges and Opportunities
Edited by Bjørn Hamre, Anne Morin and Christian Ydesen

For more information about this series, please visit: www.routledge.com/Rout ledge-Research-in-International-and-Comparative-Education/book-series/ RRICE

Home Schooling and Home Education

Race, Class and Inequality

Kalwant Bhopal and Martin Myers

LONDON AND NEW YORK

First published 2018
by Routledge
2 Park Square, Milton Park, Abingdon, Oxon OX14 4RN

and by Routledge
711 Third Avenue, New York, NY 10017

Routledge is an imprint of the Taylor & Francis Group, an informa business

© 2018 Kalwant Bhopal and Martin Myers

The right of Kalwant Bhopal and Martin Myers to be identified as author of this work has been asserted by them in accordance with sections 77 and 78 of the Copyright, Designs and Patents Act 1988.

All rights reserved. No part of this book may be reprinted or reproduced or utilised in any form or by any electronic, mechanical, or other means, now known or hereafter invented, including photocopying and recording, or in any information storage or retrieval system, without permission in writing from the publishers.

Trademark notice: Product or corporate names may be trademarks or registered trademarks, and are used only for identification and explanation without intent to infringe.

British Library Cataloguing-in-Publication Data
A catalogue record for this book is available from the British Library

Library of Congress Cataloging-in-Publication Data
A catalog record has been requested for this book

ISBN: 978-1-138-65134-0 (hbk)
ISBN: 978-1-315-62484-6 (ebk)

Typeset in Bembo
by Apex CoVantage, LLC

To our children: Dylan, Yasmin, Deva and Sachin

Contents

	Acknowledgements	viii
	Author biographies	ix
1	Introduction	1
2	Global perspectives of home education	9
3	Situating home education in global education economies	21
4	Middle-class families: 'our children do better at home'	34
5	Gypsies and Travellers: 'we have always educated our children at home'	51
6	Religion: 'we want our children to learn specific values'	67
7	Special educational needs and disability: 'most schools don't want and have never wanted our children'	83
8	Race and ethnicity: local, global or cosmopolitan identities?	102
9	Conclusions: home education, risk and belonging	118
	References	124
	Index	131

Acknowledgements

We would like to thank the families who participated in the research, for their time and willingness to speak frankly about issues that they were passionate about. We are grateful for their contribution to the study. We would also like to thank participants at seminars and conferences for the questions and discussions that this subject has generated when we have presented our research, and for comments on our blogs on the subject – this has helped in refining and generating our ideas.

Kalwant would like to thank her colleagues at the University of Birmingham, School of Education for their support. She is especially grateful to David Gillborn and Claire E. Crawford (Centre for Research in Race and Education) for their continued support and discussions which has enabled her to generate and develop her ideas.

Martin would like to raise a glass to the memory of his father Peter Myers who passed away in 2015. And, whilst he's at it he will also raise a glass to his mother Maureen Myers. Love as always to both of you.

Author biographies

Kalwant Bhopal is Professor of Education and Social Justice, Professorial Research Fellow and Deputy Director of the Centre for Research in Race and Education at the University of Birmingham, UK. Her research focuses on the achievements and experiences of minority ethnic groups in education. She has conducted research on exploring discourses of identity and intersectionality examining the lives of Black minority ethnic groups as well as examining the marginal position of Gypsies and Travellers. Her research specifically explores how processes of racism, exclusion and marginalisation operate in predominantly White spaces with a focus on social justice and inclusion. She is Visiting Professor at Harvard University in the Harvard Graduate School of Education and Visiting Professor at Kings College London (Department of Education and Professional Studies).

Martin Myers is Lecturer in Education at the University of Portsmouth. His work is primarily concerned with theorising the educational experiences of marginalised communities. In particular he has published widely about the relationships between Gypsy families, their neighbours and schools using theoretical standpoints around risk, whiteness and mobility.

1 Introduction

In 2015 and 2016 Michael Wilshaw, then Head of OFSTED[1] and HM Chief Inspector of Schools in the UK wrote on repeated occasions to the Secretary of State for Education describing his extreme concern for the safe-guarding of children who were being home educated in England (Ofsted, 2015a, 2015b, 2015c, 2016). He identified two main risks in relation to home-educated children: the first being the failure of the state to guarantee children's safety and the second, related to the first, was the failure of local authorities to monitor what happens to children after they are withdrawn from school. Whilst many other different risks are often identified in relation to home-educated children such as specific concerns about the quality of education children receive and their wider socialization, these two key concerns are almost always central to narratives around home education and home educators. They are underpinned by fundamental fears for the vulnerability of young people and fears about the vulnerability of society more generally. If education is a social process producing citizens cognizant and generally supportive of national political customs and conventions (as for example suggested in the UK's statutory guidance on teaching citizenship within the National Curriculum (DfE, 2013b)), it requires the process to be monitored, regulated and designed to give assurance about the type of citizen that is being produced and the continued safety and security of all citizens.

Michael Wilshaw's identification of child safety and the importance of monitoring are not new ideas. In the UK they were at the heart of recommendations from the earlier Badman Review (2009), the government's most thorough review of home education in the UK to date. They are also at the heart of concerns identified in other European countries (United Nations, 1989) and in the United States (NCLB, 2001). What was new in Michael Wilshaw's letter was that home education was being identified in the very specific circumstances of Muslim families' choices. Behind the general concerns of safety and invisibility was another more unsettling but less easily defined concern: one that tapped into fears generated on a global scale rather than the local concerns of local authorities. Some Muslim families it was argued were using home education as a 'cover' to radicalise their children and to promote a programme of narrow, Islamic indoctrination. Home education was suddenly not just the contested

2 Introduction

ground in which children's safety and children's rights were at stake, but was now a much wider field in which national identity was being shaped. This is unsurprising. Education has always been a part of national political identity formation and never an added extra. Situating citizenship within post-war Britain, T.H. Marshall (1990) makes a clear argument that it is the *duty* of citizens to be educated not a *right* to receive an education; education shapes and moulds the type of people we want in our society. Diane Reay (2017: 11) suggests more problematically this is a 'system that mirrors and reproduces' already existing 'hierarchical class relationships in wider society'. The process of creating citizens maintains a stasis: one in which social stability maybe prioritised but in which existing inequalities remain unchallenged and taken for granted. Home education potentially challenges the state and its citizens by allowing families to veer away from directly fulfilling their duties as citizens along predetermined routes and instead making more personal choices for their children.

This book is interested in how decisions to home educate are entangled within contested discourses often shaped by ethnicity, religion or cultural affiliations. The suspicion generated around Muslim home educators was predictable because it materialised around both a contested discourse (home education) and a minority community (Muslims) associated with alien values to the majority population. Turning our perspective 180 degrees, for minority communities mainstream schooling is often highly problematic because education, and schooling in particular, is designed to fulfil the needs of the majority. If attending school is closely linked to the duty element of citizenship, it may reasonably be associated with a means of producing a homogenous body of citizens; in doing so, it may challenge or run counter to the heterogeneous values of different families. This is one of the main reasons home education is often a strategy deployed by marginal groups in society. There is a growing body of evidence both from the United States (Fields-Smith and Williams, 2009); Mazama and Musumunu, 2014) and the UK (Bhopal and Myers, 2016) that for such families home education is often a strategy to counter racism, oppression or inequity in schools. The withdrawal of their children from schools, however, is likely to be regarded more widely as evidence of self-exclusion rather than evidence of schools and society's failing to meet their specific needs.

In many respects there is an inevitability that home education should be regarded with suspicion. In many societies the struggle for social justice is closely aligned to the struggle to acquire basic human rights – for example, the right to food and shelter so as not to be hungry and at the mercy of the elements; or the right to work rather than to be enslaved; or the right to exercise free political thought and action rather than being subservient to dictators or tyrants. Amongst such basic rights, and despite Marshall's (1990) suggestion education is simply a duty and not a right, the right to an education, to attend school independently and free of economic or cultural barriers has enormous global currency enshrined in Article 28 of the United Nations Convention on the Rights of the Child (United Nations, 1989). Home education is in many ways the epitome of a denial of a basic right; the child's right to attend school

Introduction 3

is taken away and their opportunities limited to an education shaped by their parents.

If we return to Michael Wilshaw's advice to the Secretary of State for education, we might anticipate that such a strongly worded document would result in action. The anticipation might be for greater state intervention to ensure fewer unaccounted-for children in the education system, but this has not been the case at all. In England, as in many parts of Europe and North America, there has been a significant rise in the numbers of parents who decide to home educate their children (Webb, 2010; Winstanley, 2013). This trend has not been met by increased state legislation and the reasons for this are perhaps entrenched within other narratives about home education.

Minority communities are not the only home educators. Home education is a choice made by many more typical families; the US Department for Education in its statistical survey found that 'most homeschooled students were White (83 percent) and nonpoor (89 percent)' (NCES, 2016). Often families with access to substantial economic, social and cultural capital, who want something better for their children, than what they feel is on offer from schools and the state, will make alternative provision for their children's education. Whilst more typically families with greater economic capital might choose an independent school, and in doing so, their children's education may improve dramatically whilst still remaining within the state monitoring of OFSTED or similar national monitoring bodies; for other families this is neither an option nor their best option. Some families identify failings in schools generally and missing elements in their family lives that they can change (Murphy, 2012). Such narratives are often shaped in terms of being a better family and spending time together. Not just providing better educational opportunities for children but more importantly shaping the type of family they want to be. In many respects this is a narrative that mirrors or responds directly to current neo-liberal trends towards a more marketised education system. It is a narrative in which *risks* are identified within the provision of schooling and education and families make *choices* about how they will manage those risks. In these narratives, such families are perhaps more readily identifiable as being responsible *global* citizens adapting to political and economic change in ways that are determined by rational decision-making in a rapidly changing world. The perception of other families, such as those from minority backgrounds or those with deeply held traditional beliefs, may be that they are somehow behaving less responsibly. The choices made by these families might be understood more easily as a failure to engage with a bright cosmopolitan future and, rather than embracing opportunity, fearing its consequences. In a fast-moving world the fear of being consumed within homogenous values and belief systems may become contextualised as being parochial, outdated and putting children at risk.

Home education is a context in which risk is perceived by individuals, communities and the state; and also a context in which these risks are managed by the same actors. This book explores the experiences and perceptions of different types of families who choose to manage risks they identify in

4   *Introduction*

their children's lives by home educating. There is an inevitable ambiguity at play within the perception of risk which to some extent can be understood within Ulrich Beck's account of Risk Society (1992, 2006). For Beck the distribution of risks in late modernity crosses national borders, but is managed at a very local level by individuals to shape their own lives. For home educators, risk maybe perceived in different ways: as failing schools, as cultural assimilation or as missed opportunities. However, the management of such risk is often felt to be the responsibility of the individual or the family. Home education meanwhile, is also often described in terms of being a risk in and of itself: to child safety, to child development and as a risk to the wider interests of society. The management of such risk however, does not lie with the family; it falls within a socio-political sphere in which the state enacts policies that are perceived as maintaining the rights and duties of all its citizens. In this discourse home education is a site in which there is an inevitable tension between individual, community, national and global interests. By exploring the experiences of many different groups of home educators, this book unpicks how such tensions are managed and the implications for education policy making.

Chapter outline and structure

At the heart of this book are accounts of home education by home educators. This book draws on 33 case studies with families who were home educating in England. We particularly identified certain family types in order to explore different experiences of home education, including 6 families who identified as being Muslim, 6 as being both White and middle class, 4 as Evangelical Christians, 4 families whose children had special educational needs related to disability, 8 Gypsy and Traveller and 5 Black families. Within these characteristics there were also multiple crossovers of similarly shared traits; some Black and Muslim families for example identified as being middle class and other families had strong religious beliefs.

We decided to use case study methods for our study as we were particularly interested in exploring the *reasons* why families chose to home educate. We wanted to gain a detailed understanding and analysis of why parents made this decision, particularly in relation to the positive and negative factors associated with making this decision. We wanted to provide a detailed examination of a key issue over a period of time (Hartley, 2004; Yin, 2003).

Families were accessed via specific home education organisations; this was based on contacting the organisations to arrange for adverts to be posted on their web pages asking families to participate in the research. We also contacted other organisations asking them to put us in touch with families who were home educating. After our initial contact with families, we used a snowball sample and asked respondents if they knew of other families who may be interested in participating in the study. Once we had made the initial contact, at least one parent from each family was interviewed on two separate occasions. Ethical clearance was obtained from the University of Southampton and all interview questions were piloted.

We digitally recorded and later transcribed all of the interviews. The data was analysed via an iterative process through the development of different categories where we explored different behaviours and patterns of the families and their reasons and experiences of home educating. In order to ensure accuracy and enhance validity we cross-checked our key themes and categories. We specifically organised the data based on our key research questions and our data analysis was based on 'examining, categorising, tabulating and testing' (Yin, 2003: 109). We wanted to examine specific patterns in the data in order to understand the meanings respondents gave to particular events and experiences (Neuman, 1997). Our process of data analysis consisted of three stages: drawing on theoretical propositions, exploring different explanations of these and developing descriptions of each of the cases (Yin, 2003).

The study explored how and why home education is accessed by different social groups; and secondly, how these different groups are perceived as home educators. The families in this research were, with hindsight, predictably diverse, vocal, engaged and engaging. They did not share any set of views about home education. Not only did they not have a shared understanding about how best to deliver a home education; they also did not universally agree home education was an effective means of educating children or even a 'good thing' *per se*. Within each chapter we have presented detailed accounts of two families drawn from the wider research, with similar backgrounds or reasons for choosing to home educate, but accounts that allow for a discussion of the diversity and multiplicity of viewpoints the research uncovered. To reiterate at this point, the intention of presenting contradictory accounts is not to suggest there is a right or wrong way for families to conduct themselves, rather it is intended to highlight the heterogeneity of experience. Having underlined the message of difference, it should also be noted that many similarities emerged. Some of these might be easily anticipated such as the similarity of some middle-class experience despite differences of ethnicity and religious affiliation. Others might be more surprising such as the similarities between some Gypsy family accounts and some families whose decision to home educate related to their religious background. We have also included a family who gave serious consideration to home education, but who decided eventually not to home educate, (though they did access some alternative educational provision). The decision not to home educate is of course as important as the decision to home educate: possibly what is really explored in the accounts given by many of these families are the fault-lines within state education which are readily apparent but with which many other families choose to live.

Following the introduction, Chapter 2, *Global perspectives of home education*, includes an overview of different types of home education, of the regulatory frameworks that characterise UK and United States educational policy and

6   *Introduction*

contextual detail on how home education operates in different social and political contexts. The chapter will draw on previous literature that has explored home education and provide a critical analysis of the debates and issues these foster. It will discuss how such debates are situated within the wider context of education, including globalised understandings such as the UN Convention on the Rights of the Child.

Chapter 3, *Situating home education in global education economies*, will provide a theoretical understanding of how risk might be understood in relation to home education. By drawing on the work of Ulrich Beck (1992), the chapter will explore the positioning of families who choose home education and how this is affected by race and ethnicity, class, disability and religion. The chapter will discuss how a consequence of the moral panic surrounding home education in the UK characterises it as a source of considerable 'risk' in children's lives, particularly in relation to marginal or non-mainstream families (Beck, 1992). It will make a central argument that in societies that become more cosmopolitan (Beck, 2006), the positioning of certain groups, particularly more marginalised communities or groups who are disengaged from the mainstream, become further side-lined. In the context of home educators, their choices become identified with introducing risk into their children's lives. This is ironic on a number of levels, not least because the more marginalised home educators in our research tended to be the families faced with more pressing risks in their children's lives. More mainstream families were more likely to be considered as making strategic or 'lifestyle' choices to manage the 'risks' they faced.

Chapter 4, *Middle-class families: 'our children do better at home'*, explores the experiences of middle-class families who have chosen home education for their children. It will draw upon the accounts of two families who defined themselves as middle class and who chose home education. Both families highlighted issues that perhaps are common to many home educators; they were dissatisfied with local schools and felt they could provide a better alternative. However, their accounts also identify other motivations often focused on the type of family experience they wanted their children to experience and a sense that the parent's lifestyle could also be improved. This chapter also discusses the deployment of economic, social and cultural capital by middle-class families.

Chapter 5, *Gypsies and Travellers: 'we have always educated our children at home'*, focuses on the experiences of Gypsy families for whom home education is often considered a traditional or normal route to acquiring an education. It specifically examines the experiences of such families in relation to the cultural norms and values of Gypsy and Traveller communities. It explores the discourses by which home education is negotiated in relation to schooling, and how Gypsies, who are already positioned as a marginalised group, maybe identified as further excluding themselves in the process of choosing home education (unlike the middle-class families discussed in the preceding chapter).

Chapter 6, *Religion: 'we want our children to learn specific values'*, explores the experiences of an evangelical Christian and a Muslim family who chose to

Introduction 7

home educate. In part for both families this was a means of delivering an education that promoted their cultural values and more widely maintained and developed bonding social capital within their communities. Both families felt to a greater or lesser extent their religion identified their children as being different in mainstream schools, (and for one family was a direct source of racism). The chapter discusses how the implications of such an education may work to exclude these children from becoming full citizens in society.

Chapter 7, *Special educational needs and disability: 'most schools do not want, and never have wanted, our children'*, highlights the concerns of families whose children have special needs or disabilities for whom home education has often represented an alternative to state schooling. The two families in this chapter provide some rich insights into some of the reasons home education is more widely seen to be attractive, including the identification of the importance of the 'home' in home education. The two families in this chapter both identified special needs related to their children's disabilities and their accounts of home education related directly to their children's needs. More generally a constant feature in our research was family's identification of their child as 'special'. The connection between the intimacy of the home, of the importance of family and the provision of tailored education are discussed in detail.

Chapter 8, *Race and ethnicity: local, global or cosmopolitan identities?* is the final findings chapter and in many respects it brings together the themes raised in earlier chapters including dissatisfaction with schools, experiences of racism, difference and the desire for children to have secure and successful futures. It describes the experiences and choices of two Black families living in London. For these families very specific risks materialised in relation to race and schooling. Despite equalities policies and despite the impression of schools being multicultural institutions, both families identified huge failings in the education their children received. They discuss how their global perspectives on risk and experiences of migration shaped their family identities within local community settings and influenced their decision-making. This chapter includes the account of one family who shared many of the misgivings associated with local schools that led other families to decide to home educate. However despite such misgivings and despite giving serious consideration to home education, they eventually chose to remain with the school and not to home educate. They did however access alternative Saturday Schools in which children's Black identities were supported and they drew heavily on social capital within family networks and local churches. The other family in this chapter highlight another account of home education in which they felt their family was pushed, by the school and local authority, to choose home education because they were identified as being a problematic or 'difficult' family based on their ethnicity and class.

The book concludes with Chapter 9, *Home education, risk and belonging*, which debates the wider context of how home education is understood in terms of citizenship, belonging and difference. It considers how risk is assigned

8   Introduction

differently in relation to different communities who choose to home educate, and how risk is often understood in racialized and classed terms in the context of home education.

Note

1 OFSTED is the Office for Standards in Education, children's services and skills. Its role is to inspect and regulate services that care for children and young people in the UK.

2 Global perspectives of home education

One impact of globalisation and increasingly neo-liberal economies has been the trend towards the creation of a Global Education Industry or GEI in which greater private investment within traditionally state-run education practices is also matched by increasingly market-driven practice in the state sector's delivery of education (Verger et al., 2016). At the same time there has been another, perhaps related, global tendency to move towards a normative school model; this reflects in part the increasing demand for children's global rights including the right to an education. Articles 28 and 29 of The United Nations Convention on the Rights of the Child (United Nations, 1989) seemingly presuppose education being delivered in school settings. It is then perhaps surprising that home-educating families are not only found in countries across the world but also that they often appear to be a growing phenomenon in Western developed nations. Also surprising is the considerable range and variation found in the regulation, legislation and rules applicable to home education to be found not just between different countries but between different states or regional areas in the same country. Home education may well be one setting in which global citizens defined by shared rights and values are not immediately identifiable.

This chapter briefly explores the different regulatory structures that are encountered before considering who home educates, why they choose to do so and how effective a practice it might be. In part what underscores such an examination, and what is explored in greater detail in the case studies presented in later chapters, is very much a picture in which lots of different people are doing lots of different things in lots of different contexts: heterogeneity rules! It is worth flagging up the very local practices of many home educators adapting to global education practice is indicative of a cosmopolitan lifestyle, in which individuals manage risks that stretch far beyond their national borders (Beck, 1992, 2006).

Regulation and legislation

Home educators or homeschoolers[1] are confronted by a wide array of different legislation largely dependent on their geographical location. Primarily this determines whether or not home education is legal where they live and levels of monitoring and regulation by the state.

10 *Global perspectives of home education*

United States

In the United States until 1980 homeschooling was effectively illegal in the majority of states; this changed progressively on a state by state basis, and it was only in 1993 that it became legal in all states (Basham et al., 2007; Cooper and Sureau, 2007; Gaither, 2008). One noticeable consequence being that different states maintain different regimes of regulation and monitoring and no national guidelines exist. The differences between states can be quite stark; some states effectively do not regulate at all and do not require parents to inform them of their decision, whilst other states can be grouped within low, moderate and high regulatory regimes (Lips and Feinberg, 2008). In low regulation states parents need to inform education departments they are homeschooling. Moderate states require parents to inform their education department they are homeschooling and send updates on children's test scores or alternative evaluations of progress. In high regulation states additional evidence of the curriculum, home visits or evidence of parental qualifications are required. In 25 states there is either no regulation or low regulation of homeschooling and high regimes of regulation are only identifiable in 10 states (Lips and Feinberg, 2008).

Ray and Eagleson (2008) suggest that if homeschooling is to be regulated on a national scale, this would need to address the different philosophical, academic, human development and socio-political reasons behind parental decisions to home educate. Such an approach might suggest a myriad of competing and potentially irreconcilable parental (and potential voter) voices. Examples of interest convergence however are noted to materialise around issues of funding and cost. Apple (2015) suggests Christian conservative homeschoolers have become 'adept at taking advantage of government resources' (2015: 288) by modelling their homeschooling as enrolment in Charter schools; whilst simultaneously, cash-strapped districts can benefit from the associated influx of state funding following dramatic increases in enrolment in Charter schools (Huerta, 2000). Such cynical manoeuvring around legislation and regulatory frameworks is noticeably subject to criticism by homeschoolers themselves and their advocates, such as the Home School Legal Defense Association (HSLDA), who regard Charter schools and Virtual schools as delivering too much state interference in private family life (Miron et al., 2013). For homeschoolers guided by ideological positions in which the privacy of family life is privileged over state intrusion, public funding is inevitably problematic because it leads to questions of accountability and the need for regulation. Whilst Apple (2007) notes the movement of public funding towards non-traditional engagement in public schooling by Christian conservative homeschoolers associated with an ideological political shift to the right, others have countered homeschooling represents a saving of taxpayer money (Belfield, 2005).

Canada

Homeschooling is legal in all 10 Canadian provinces but as in the United States there are differences in the level of regulation varying from no or low regulation to moderate regulation (Donnelly, 2012). In most provinces parents have to register their children as being homeschooled or submit a formal application to inform the local education authority that they are doing so (Hepburn and Van Belle, 2003). The main objective for regulation in Canada is that homeschooled children should receive a 'satisfactory' home education; however Donnelly suggests that 'while there may be certain state controls present in an actual home schooling environment, the bottom line is that the parent, not the state, is in charge and responsible for providing their child's education' (2012: 210).

Europe and the European Union

Just as individual states are not bound by a national framework, similarly in Europe and even within the European Union, there is no single regulatory framework for home educators. The European Union has tended to promote broadly homogenous policy such as encouraging greater secondary school completion; fostering the provision of education for families who cross national boundaries; but still allowing for local flexibility in terms of provision including for home education (Koons, 2010). Petrie (1995, 2001) notes a small shift towards greater accommodation by member states for home educators identifying a spectrum of different regulation. At one end of this spectrum are countries who have a history of allowing home education, (including the UK, Ireland, France and the Scandinavian countries); countries (including Austria and Hungary) where home education has more recently been allowed; and, countries where either home education is not allowed or is permitted in a small number of exceptional cases (including Germany, Spain and Portugal). Outside of the EU, Kostelecká (2010) notes the move towards legalising home education in a large number of post-communist states and again identifies the different approaches to regulation that emerge within different states.

United Kingdom

The UK has been identified as having a very light touch approach in its regulation of home educators (Bhopal and Myers, 2016). Section 7 of the 1944 Education Act (later superseded by the 1996 Education Act) outlines the 'duty' of parents to ensure children of compulsory school age receive a 'suitable' education; however, there is no requirement this should happen in a school setting. The exact wording of the Act as it currently stands is as follows:

> The parent of every child of compulsory school age shall cause him to receive efficient full-time education suitable –
>
> (a) to his age, ability and aptitude, and
> (b) to any special educational needs he may have, either by regular attendance at school or otherwise.
>
> (Education Act, 1996, Part 1, Chapter 1, Section 7)

12 *Global perspectives of home education*

The Act reflected a post-war spirit embodied in the cross-party support for the Beveridge Report. The emphasis is on a national duty to ensure children are educated rather than education being a right (reflecting Marshall's (1950) concurrent accounts of citizenship); and, possibly reflecting the urgency of rebuilding and repositioning the nation, it seemingly lacks detail. In the 1980s the concept of what constitutes a 'suitable' education was challenged; resulting in a high court ruling that still seemed to struggle to pin down a clear-cut meaning. It settled instead on loosely defining such an education as one that prepares a child for life in a modern civilised society and to achieve their full potential (Bhopal and Myers, 2016). Similarly the definition of education is left hanging in the air in the phrase 'otherwise'; the act does not define what that 'otherwise' might or might not include. The significance of this phrasing has not been lost on home educators in the UK who cite the ill-defined space of 'otherwise' to demonstrate their abidance with the law. One of the earliest home education charities and self-help groups, Education Otherwise, even adopted it for their name.

If schools believe that children are not attending school for a legitimate reason, their local authority can issue a School Attendance Order, and if this is the case parents can then be prosecuted (OFSTED, 2010). However, the monitoring and enforcement of home educators is hampered in large part by the lack of national guidelines; local authorities are expected to draw up their own guidance for home educators in their area. Whilst the Department for Education (DfE, 2013a) recommended these should include a policy statement about home education and guidance to parents, the detail is left to individual authorities and there is no specific requirement to compile a register of home educators or to monitor the quality of education they are delivering. Education Otherwise and other home education organisations regularly cite guidance to the effect that 'parents are not legally required to give the LEA access to their home or their child', and that the 'current legal situation in the UK with regard to home education can be summarised in the phrase, "Education is compulsory, schooling is not"' (Bhopal and Myers, 2016; Education Otherwise, 2017).

Foster suggests that although local authorities have duties 'to identify children not receiving a suitable education, and to intervene if a child is not receiving a suitable education' (2015: 4), it is not a requirement for them to specifically monitor home educators and their provision of education. Similar concerns were highlighted in the most wide-ranging government review of home education, the Badman Review (Badman, 2009) and more recently by OFSTED (2015b).

South America, Asia, Australia

The countries that permit homeschooling and monitor the educational process of those who are homeschooling include Australia and New Zealand. In Israel parents are not in principle allowed to home school but educational authorities often make exceptions to this rule. In Argentina, Brazil and Cuba compulsory school attendance is required and homeschooling is not allowed.

Who home educates and why

The range of regulatory frameworks and different requirements for monitoring in different countries and states creates difficulties when trying to establish the numbers or characteristics of home educators. Furthermore one identifiable trend is the diversity of home educators both in terms of their ideological or religious beliefs (Apple, 2015); the narratives associated with individual family choices (Rothermel, 2011, 2015); and social differences such as class, ethnicity or religion (Apple, 2015; Gaither, 2008).

This is exacerbated to some extent by doubts that have regularly surfaced concerning the validity of much research that has examined home education. These include concerns about a tendency towards small-scale qualitative studies, using self-selected samples, (Lines, 2000; Medlin, 2000); failing to distinguish between student performance and the effects of home education (Belfield, 2004; Medlin, 2000); inadequate control for socio-economic variables such as income, class and occupation (Dahlquist et al., 2006); and little research around children's perspectives (Schemmer, 1985). In addition Kunzman (2009) notes evidence of misrepresentation of sampling sizes and frames in some research portraying a positive interpretation of home education.

Murphy (2012: 13) suggests, 'One of the most stark conclusions one draws when reviewing the scholarly literature on home schooling is just how thin the empirical knowledge base is on this social phenomenon and educational movement'. In part this relates to the challenges of conducting research with people outside of traditional institutional structures, who may not necessarily be engaged in similar or comparable education practices, who may deploy a mix of traditional schooling and home education, and who may adopt different practices at different times (Jones-Sanpei, 2008; Wilkens et al., 2015). Isenberg highlights the difficulties in particular of understanding the progress of home-schooled students due to high attrition rates over often relatively short periods of time (Isenberg, 2016, 2007).

Beyond the methodological problems, Wilkens highlights the 'politicisation' of home education research, noting that much of the 'available scholarship has been conducted or published by advocacy organisations or by scholars with explicit agendas to promote or criticise home schooling' (Wilkens, 2015: 32). Too much research runs the risk of either presenting a rose-tinted perspective of flexible teaching and learning practice enabling strong family bonding, individualisation and high academic achievement; or alternatively, highlighting the dangers of inadequate teaching practice, neglect and abuse, lack of achievement and a lack of socialisation (Bhopal and Myers, 2016).

Homeschooling in the United States

Homeschooling is not a new phenomenon in the United States and predominated throughout its early colonial and postcolonial history (Gaither, 2008). It was essentially the normal practice of education until the nineteenth century

14 *Global perspectives of home education*

when social and political change associated with industrialisation and urbanisation marked a shift toward democratic politics and increasing state involvement in the provision of social welfare at an institutional level rather than through traditional family practice (Katz, 1987). From the 1870s compulsory attendance was legislated for within institutionally recognised schools with a professional recognised body of teachers (Basham et al., 2007). This model of education was generally accepted until the late 1970s when different groups of parents began to press for legalisation of homeschooling. Stevens (2001, 2003) notes the rapidity with which homeschooling transformed itself from being an unusual and marginal activity into an accepted and well-established practice. Homeschooling in America was driven by two contrary ideological positions in the late 1970s – on the one hand the liberal left and on the other the Christian right. Stevens (2001) notes that despite their very obvious political and religious differences, many on both sides have tended to portray themselves as having unconventional or individualistic approaches to daily life. That arguments around homeschooling often play out within ideological terms tends to support Murphy's assertion that they need to be considered within 'an ongoing debate about who should control the education of America's children, government or parents' (Murphy, 2012: 60) in which the presumed dominance of professional, pedagogical expertise is contested locally and at a grassroots level by parents.

The Christian right, Protestant and evangelical in nature, has largely come to be seen as the dominant 'face' of American homeschooling (Arai, 2000), shaping it in a context that understands morality in stark contradictions between good and evil and characterised by privileging parental authority over children's rights in which the 'family, not the child held centre stage' (Arai, 2000: 35). For the Christian right the institutional and public provision of education rather than private, family-centred lives represents 'a contest between personal rights and freedoms held up against the power of the state to control the individual' (Cooper and Sureau, 2007).

The libertarian left was typified by the work of John Holt who promoted 'unschooling' (Holt, 1969; Moore and Moore, 1994). Holt argued that public schools were essentially bad for children and did not adapt to their individual learning journeys (Holt, 1969, 1982). Consequently, a group who became known as the 'unschoolers' wanted their children's individual needs to be at the centre of their learning and argued that this learning should take place in a flexible learning environment. Holt was responsible for publishing one of the first newsletters, *Growing Without Schooling*, aimed at supporting homeschoolers and in doing so was an early example of homeschooling becoming an effective social movement. Stevens (2003) suggests this element of building effective social networks has been key to the greater and more prolonged success of Christian Right homeschoolers. He notes the importance of the organisational and entrepreneurial strengths of organisations such as the Home School Legal Defence Association (HSLDA) to promote both the interests of homeschoolers and, despite tax-exempt, charitable status, their own financial interests.

There has been a proliferation of support groups since the 1970s. Whilst some of these have been organised within local geographical settings as small-scale self-help groups (Lubeke, 1999), or those which promote 'mix and meet' opportunities for children (Lubeke, 1999), more prominent examples abound that work at the state or national level often focused on supporting Christian families (Cibulka, 1991; Murphy, 2012). Such groups, like the HSLDA, have promoted homeschooling through political campaigning and legal defence work. Many other support networks grew to provide curriculum support, educational resources and materials for parents (Mayberry et al., 1995). Apple (2006a, 2015) notes the importance of the '*organizational form*' that materialises, 'since much of the religiously conservative homeschooling movement has a sense of purity and danger in which all elements of the world have a set place, such an organization of both knowledge and pedagogy embodies the ideological structure underlying the evangelical universe' (2015: 294). This amalgam of religion, politics and business promotes both a grassroots feel and sense of individualism rooted in deeply held convictions that are organisationally highly effective, with Stevens (2002) going as far as to suggest the drift towards right-wing American politics in many respects reflects the organisational strength of Christian Protestants seen in action as homeschoolers.

From being positioned as a marginal activity often regarded with scepticism and suspicion (Knowles et al., 1992; Stevens, 2003), homeschooling has grown considerably and is now seen as part of mainstream education (Reich, 2005) and American society (Basham et al., 2007). One consequence of this shift has been the inclusion of questions about its practice being included in census data and how homeschooling should be regulated. Murphy suggests that since the 1990s the question of whether homeschooling should be legalised ceased to be an issue and has been superseded by a debate over 'the extent to which home schooling should be controlled by the state' (Murphy, 2012: 45). Key, and often controversial, issues include regulation of homeschooler's curriculum, student assessment, testing and examinations, time spent learning and who should be qualified to homeschool (Dahlquist et al., 2006). Homeschoolers themselves, though often well-organised, do not necessarily present a unified voice. Some groups lobbying to ensure homeschoolers (and the rights of families) were included in the *No Child Left Behind* policy (Ray, 2005), whilst others actively campaigned to distance themselves (and avoid requirements for testing) (Somerville, 2005).

The National Center for Education Statistics (NCES), the federal body tasked with gathering and analysing educational data in the United States, identified a significant rise from just under 1 to 1.8 million homeschooled children between 1999 and 2012, representing an increase from 1.7% to 3.4% of the total school population (Redford et al., 2016). However, this number appears to have levelled out, and in 2017, 1.7 million children (3.3% of the total school population) were identified as homeschooled (Grady, 2017). Discussing the history of homeschooling, Gaither (2008) suggests that the population of those who participate in homeschooling today is more heterogeneous than previously

16 *Global perspectives of home education*

thought, with those from a diverse range of ethnic, religious and social backgrounds deciding to do so. These include growing numbers of Muslim families (McKeon, 2007), and Black and Latino families (Apple, 2006b; Fields-Smith, 2016; Musumunu and Mazama, 2015; Taylor, 2005), though often their experiences are under-researched. Kunzman (2009) also argues that beyond religious and ideological grounds, there is great diversity in the characteristics of homeschoolers. Despite this, the NCES data still suggests most 'homeschooled students were White (83 percent) and nonpoor (89 percent)' (Redford et al., 2016: ii). Some evidence suggests homeschoolers tend to have high levels of education or a college education (Sutton and Bogan, 2005), to be financially secure and from middle class socio-economic backgrounds (Belfield, 2004) and that mothers are more likely than fathers to have responsibility for homeschooling (Apple, 2015; Stevens, 2001). There is evidence (supported by the NCES data) that homeschooling is often adopted by families whose children have disabilities (Duvall, 2005). Religious families, particularly Protestant evangelicals, are more likely to homeschool (Lines, 1991; McKeon, 2007; Ray, 1997).

Whilst religious and ideological reasons remain an important factor (Gaither, 2008; Planty et al., 2009),

> increasing numbers who opt to home school do so as an accessory, hybrid, temporary stop gap, or out of necessity given their circumstances, and it is this newer group of home schoolers who are challenging the historic dichotomies between public and private, school and home, formal and informal that have played an important role in the movement's self-definition and in American education.
>
> (Gaither, 2008: 343)

This is borne out by the NCES data which identified a range of reasons given as 'important' and 'most important' for choosing homeschooling. Whilst providing religious instruction (64%) or moral instruction (77%) was found to be important, factors found to be of more significance were concerns around drugs, peer pressure and safety in schools (91%) and dissatisfaction with academic instruction (74%). When asked what the 'most important' reason was for choosing homeschooling, concerns about drugs, peer pressure and safety in schools was the most cited reason (25%) followed by dissatisfaction with academic instruction (19%), whilst providing religious instruction was cited by 17% of parents (Planty et al., 2009). If nothing else, such data highlights that parental decisions are based around managing many concerns about their children's education and not necessarily driven in response to one issue.

Homeschooling in Canada

As in the United States, there is evidence of increasing numbers of families choosing to homeschool (Basham et al., 2007). Research conducted in Canada suggests that many parents are dissatisfied with public schooling and regard

Global perspectives of home education   17

homeschooling as a strategy to exercise greater control over the values being taught and to tailoring their children's education to their individual needs (Van Pelt, 2003). Specific reasons identified by parents for homeschooling often mirror the mix of academic concerns, family values and personal beliefs typical of American homeschoolers (Basham et al., 2007). These include concerns about poor learning environments in schools, often described in terms of a lack of discipline in public schools. Whilst private education is regarded as one means of ensuring children learn in safer environments, the prohibitive cost of such a strategy has encouraged parents to adopt a homeschool approach instead. Objections to the curriculum both in terms of the lack of a religious education and the failure to deliver high quality academic outcomes are regularly cited. Family reasons tend to focus on the desire to build better and stronger relationships between parents and children.

The characteristics of families who homeschool are also similar to those found in the United States; they tend to be two-parent families and home-schooled children tend to perform better academically than those who attend public schools (Van Pelt, 2003). There is also research to suggest that children who are homeschooled – far from being isolated – participate in a great deal of extra curriculum activities which includes visits outside of the home (Van Pelt, 2003). Basham et al. suggest that although 'home schooling is neither desirable nor possible for all families, it has proven itself to be a relatively inexpensive and successful educational alternative' (2007: 19).

Home education in the UK

As in North America, homeschooling is a growing trend in the UK; however despite sharing some features, there are noticeable differences. The lack of regulation in the UK has meant there is very little reliable data on which to estimate numbers of children being homeschooled – a concern highlighted in both the Badman Review (2009) and more recently by then Chief Inspector of Schools, Michael Wilshaw (Ofsted, 2015b). Badman (2009) suggested there may be as many as 80,000 children being educated outside of school and it has been suggested the actual figure maybe twice that (Fortune-Wood, 2005). However, estimates based on freedom of information requests sent to Local Authorities have placed the numbers around the 37,000 mark (Jeffreys, 2015; Mansell and Edwards, 2016). One specific difference in the UK is the use of nomenclature with homeschooling described in official contexts as 'home education' or more specifically 'elective home education'. In many respects such nomenclature underpins the distinction made in the 1996 Education Act requiring parents to provide an education for children but not to attend schools. It also usefully draws attention to the distinction between education as a broader concept embracing wide-ranging philosophies around development rather than the specific work of schools.

Amongst the most identifiable differences between home education in the UK and homeschooling in North America is that it is not a practice

18 *Global perspectives of home education*

overwhelmingly associated with Conservative Christianity; and, despite clear signs of growth in commercial educational support economies, it still remains a comparatively non-commercial practice. Families often belong to local support groups, there are very effective advocacy groups such as Education Otherwise and commercially produced curriculum materials and self-help guides are easily available: none of these however are as dominant a feature as in the United States.

Reasons for choosing to home educate are wide-ranging (Rothermel, 2015; Smith and Nelson, 2015). Parental concerns about the quality of education in schools and a belief they can do better themselves are often contextualised within narratives of increasing pressure placed on children through the introduction of testing regimes at all ages in schools (Rothermel, 2015; Webb, 2010). Often associated with concerns about pressure is the belief that a more relaxed, child-centric approach to learning is one in which closer bonds between families are nurtured (Hopwood et al., 2007), one in which 'the most important aspect of a child's learning is that the child should be learning for the sake of it, for the intrinsic pleasure in finding things out and discovering the world around him' (Webb, 2010: 30). The importance of 'the home' in home education, as a space in which the significance of the family is defined, has perhaps been overlooked in debates about home education (Kraftl, 2013). Kraftl (2013) highlights how for home educators the relationship between family and education is fostered within the intimacy of home spaces. As in the United States differences in values and belief systems, often but not exclusively associated with religious faith, determine many family's decisions to home educate. Specific poor experiences of schools such as children being bullied or subject to racism are also often identified as significant in parent's decision-making (Bhopal and Myers, 2016; Gabb, 2004).

Certain groups and communities are often associated with home education, including families whose children have Special Educational Needs. Their reasons for choosing home education often reflect their concerns that schools are not able to provide the type of education suitable for their children. However, such parents also invariably cite more nuanced accounts of their decision that encompasses wider reasons, perhaps around their personal family ethos or around experiences of bullying. The tendency for families to have complex narratives about their choices is reflected more generally. Gypsy and Traveller families in the UK for example are often home educators (Bhopal and Myers, 2016; D'Arcy, 2014; Ivatts, 2006), but their reasons for doing so are often more complex than is given credence in public discourses that characterise such families as simply avoiding sending their children to school. Gypsy families for example often draw upon a very traditional view of education in which the skills required to be economically successful are transferred intergenerationally. At the same time schooling is often identified with a loss of culture at the expense of gaining new skills, and the experience of accessing schools is often marked by extreme hostility and racism directed towards Gypsy children. Against such a backdrop it is also noticeable that many Gypsy families will

Global perspectives of home education 19

identify the importance and intimacy of their home as very significant in determining the choices made for their families. What is noticeable is that whilst Gypsy families are often identified as being different or outsiders in relation to the wider population, these more nuanced accounts often reflect the same or similar dilemmas faced by many other home educators. In the case studies used in this book, many of these dilemmas are explored in greater detail.

Risk and home education

Understandings of home education in the UK have been shaped by specific concerns about risk – in particular the risk posed by children not attending school and being educated in the home. Understandably home educators have found the suggestion that they place their children at risk a highly provocative argument. It is an argument that is entrenched in often misleading binaries: distinctions between child and parental rights; education as a societal or individual project; or between religious and secular values. It is also true to say it is sometimes home educators themselves who place the debate within such misleading arguments, for example by making the argument that social policy designed to protect child well-being and safety is not just intrusive within family life but also, simultaneously identifies *all* home educators as putting their children at risk. How we might wish to problematise and understand risk is discussed at greater length in the next chapter; it is useful however to foreground how risk related to child safety has been associated with home education.

There have been a number of high-profile media accounts of child abuse in the UK in which home education has either been cited as the main or a contributory cause to that abuse going undetected. One of the most significant from the perspective of understanding attitudes towards home education was the death of Khyra Ishaq in 2008. She was a 7-year-old Black girl living in the West Midlands whose parents allowed her to starve to death. At the time social services in the West Midlands had concerns about her welfare and attempted to make home visits but were denied access to the family home on a number of occasions. One reason given for the family being able to deny access was that the mother told the Local Authority they were home educating. One direct consequence of this tragedy was the wide-ranging governmental investigation of home education led by Graham Badman and subsequent publication of 'The Badman Review' (Badman, 2009). The key foci of the review included investigating the barriers that existed for local authorities and social services to carry out their roles effectively; whether local authorities were providing the right support for families who were home educating; whether changes should be made to the then current Every Child Matters policy and whether home education could be used as a cover for child abuse in the home.

The Badman Review made a number of recommendations which acknowledged that home education and its lack of consistent regulation and monitoring in the UK could pose potential risks to some home-educated children. These included 'a compulsory national registration scheme, locally administered for all

20 *Global perspectives of home education*

children of statutory school age, who are, or become electively home educated' (2009: 47). Such a scheme would require an annual local registration by parents choosing to home educate their children. Another recommendation was for a review of what should be understood by a 'suitable' and 'efficient' education as defined in the Education Act 1996 and related to current education policy. This demonstrates how 'risk' is quickly identified not just in terms of physical well-being or safety but also in terms of anticipating education as a means of socialisation and becoming productive in terms of wider societal values and expectation. Badman recommended local authorities should have a right of access to the home when parents are home educating and a right to speak to the child alone if the local authority thinks it is appropriate. The review made other recommendations largely related to researching further and understanding the choices and decisions made by home educators and putting in place greater support mechanisms for them.

The Badman Review was a crucial moment in identifying and associating specific 'risks' with home educators. However, its key recommendations were never implemented. The Labour government's Education Secretary Ed Balls attempted to include the recommendations made by Badman within an Education Bill, but was unable to do so, in part because in the run-up to a general election, a very successful advocacy campaign was conducted by home educators which resulted in new legislation being delayed. The new Coalition government of Conservatives and Liberal Democrats did not attempt to introduce these changes. In many ways although 'risk' was identified in both the specific sense of well-being and safety and also as a more general expectation of what education should do for society, it was a moment in which understandings of 'home educators' and risk became more delineated. 'Risk' appeared to be identified with particular types of home educators (Bhopal and Myers, 2016). In the tragedy of Khyra Ishaq's death, narratives of poor, underclass families putting their children at risk emerge. This has been a trend that has continued with Gypsy families often identified as using home education as a 'cover' in order to avoid sending their children to school and Muslim families using home education as a 'cover' for radicalising their children (Bhopal and Myers, 2016; Myers and Bhopal, 2018). In many ways this is strange; the 'risk' of home education seems unavoidably interlinked with the mechanics of its process: within family management and decision-making as played out against education and welfare policies. However, the narratives of 'risk' that emerge invariably appear to focus on *who* home educates rather than *how* they home educate.

Note

1 'Home education' and 'home educators' are terms typically used in the UK whilst 'home-schooling' and 'home schoolers' are typically used in the United States and elsewhere.

3 Situating home education in global education economies

There is an outsized question at the heart of any discussion about home education or homeschooling; and, in part the reason it has become such an outsized question is that it is largely unanswered. That question, posed in the most naked fashion would be: is home education a good thing?

Some of the reasons it remains unanswered can be ascertained from the previous chapter which highlighted how fragmented a topic home education is; how home education varies not just from country to country, but from household to household, from family to family. It has different names: homeschooling in the United States and many other countries; home education in the UK, but also sometimes elective home education; sometimes unschooling; and, sometimes alternative schooling. The question raises uncertainties about what is being measured; should home education be judged on academic outcomes or social outcomes? Is any of the data around outcomes and progression into further education or employment credible? Is it to be assessed against the rights of children? Of parents? Of families? Are these ever the same thing? Are 'schooling' and 'education' one and the same? Is it relevant to compare individual private lives against the education policies of the state? Of other social policies? Against human rights? Can it be measured against the needs of society? Of delivering good citizens?

Drawing on Ulrich Beck's (1992) account of 'risk society', this chapter explores the positioning of families who chose home education as a means of managing risk. As discussed in the previous chapter, throughout the latter part of the twentieth century and the beginning of the twenty-first century, education has increasingly been understood from a global perspective. This is unsurprising as many aspects of daily life are increasingly understood within more globalised perspectives; and, for education, might be perceived in the not necessarily aligned movements towards normative schooling models, increasing assertions of global human rights and a shift towards commodified education economies reflecting the ascendancy of neo–liberalism. For individuals and families such global trends have real impacts on their daily lives – impacts that often need to be managed at a very local level. They are impacts that are often experienced around local intersectionalities around race and ethnicity, class and religion. Such intersectionalities regularly delineate the moments where the interests of societies and individuals do not align. Homogenous models of education are not necessarily effective in understanding the heterogeneous circumstances of different families. And, at the same time, that some families choose home education because they find it difficult to manage their belonging to a wider spectrum of society than people within their own close family and social networks. Risk here becomes quickly entangled in discourses around citizenship, an equation in which home educators might be seen to privilege their personal rights over their social duties.

At such moments the management of 'risk' is also pertinent to home education precisely because 'risk' is identified as being introduced into children's lives when they are home educated. Home educators, positioned outside of the mainstream and normative regimes of schooling, are identifiable as potentially responsible for causing risk, rather than managing it. This has been particularly evidenced in the UK where the trigger for the most far-reaching review of home education was the death of a home-educated child (Badman, 2009) and the heightened interest of the schools inspection body, OFSTED, was initiated following concerns of Islamic radicalisation (Myers and Bhopal, 2018). Such intense interest around particular issues (e.g. child abuse, physical harm) and around particular more marginal or non-mainstream communities (e.g. Muslims), often has the hallmarks of a 'moral panic' (Cohen, 1972). In particular the disproportionality of interest in public discourse seems to be generated around intersectionalities of certain groups of people and certain types of events, rather than home education *per se*. What emerges is a disjunct between families who potentially manage their perception of themselves in a global setting in which the risk of an inadequate or inappropriate education for their children is all too real; against a societal perception of very local and specific risks often perceived in an exaggerated fashion driven by media interest.

Managing risk

Beck's (1992) description of 'risk society' identifies a historic shift in which individuals take greater responsibility for managing risks in their lives. Throughout late modernity risks are increasingly identified as being transnational, driven by global rather than local events. Whilst in the past 'risks' associated with education may have been determined by social class, geographical location or the political leanings of ideologically inclined social policies, increasingly parents are faced by the requirement to make their own choices about what sort of education will best serve their children. Such a shift can be seen in terms of the move towards a neo-liberal education in which schools and universities are characterised as markets in which parents and students makes choices about how to invest in their education. In this context home education could be identified as a natural choice, freely made by some parents; in other words one choice amongst many that emerge through the education market. The claims for a free-market in which education can take place unfettered by government interference are belied by the evidence suggesting government is actually acutely aware and willing to interfere in *some* families' choices. Describing the growth in state activity to reduce welfare payments and massively increase incarceration, Wacquant notes how economic understandings of neo-liberalism as a hands-off, free-market enterprise are 'thin and incomplete' (Wacquant, 2010: 213). Behind the smokescreen of light touch economic policy is the heavy hand of the state directing and manipulating social controls that inevitably identify racial minorities and the poor as blameworthy, whilst providing security and privileging the interests of the wealthy and powerful. It is the economic successes of elites that require draconian and punitive state interference and not failing economic cycles or increasing crime rates.

Risk and citizenship

Risk and perceptions of risk emerge consistently within discourses about home education. In part this reflects the obvious framing of child welfare concerns within expectations of state interventions to protect children. There are commonly held understandings that any form of education or schooling, including home education, should reflect both professional expertise of welfare and educational practice, whilst still acknowledging the very particular interests and rights that parents and children possess (Webb, 2010). Webb (2010) suggests a range of specific approaches that would acknowledge the rights of children to access a good quality education including an ongoing relationship between local authorities and home-educating families. Parents would be expected to produce a plan of their proposed educational intentions and be held accountable for its effective delivery; and, children would also be assured of rights to sit public exams. Local authorities would also be expected to provide greater resources for home educators, suggesting a correlation in many respects between the duties and rights of being a citizen that mirrors mainstream schooling. It is fair to say that many home educators, including advocacy groups such as Education Otherwise, would find such an approach far too intrusive.

There are also wider discourses in which the production of a cohesive society is understood to be shaped by the education and schooling of young people and such approaches would argue the balance of interventions should shift away from the family and further towards the state and wider community. Reich (2005) argues there is a legitimate need for regulation for homeschooling, (including registration schemes, monitoring what is being taught and how successfully), related to the need to protect the incipient freedoms associated with young people becoming citizens. Such freedoms relate to the wider body of citizens instilling a civic education and shared values; in this sense the state is not acting in an intrusive or interfering fashion but simply reflecting the wider shared values of its members. Democracy is fundamentally threatened if home-educated children,

> can be sheltered and isolated in a way that students in schools, even sectarian private schools cannot be. Parents can limit opportunities for social

24 *Situating home education in global education*

interaction, control the curriculum and create a learning environment in which the values of parents are replicated and reinforced in every possible way.

(Reich, 2005: 114)

Reich (2005) suggests that if good public schools were available to all parents, those parents who choose to home educate their children would still take this option. Many parents who home educate their children do so for different reasons than simply to ensure they receive the highest academic standards, (though for many parents this is their main or a significant factor). Beyond the realm of academic achievement, Reich identifies the desire for parents to exercise greater control of not just the effectiveness of learning, but also how it is done and the contexts in which it takes place. One measure of different types of welfare state is the level of decommodification around the delivery of services including education (Esping-Andersen, 2013); that is to say to what extent does the state intervene in economies rather than allow market economics free reign. In more decommodified states the rights of the citizen are perhaps more closely monitored and shaped by the state and by other citizens. The adoption of home education is a very individualised response to education provision in which the family invests its own resources in order to deliver education. In many respects this is close to the absolute commodification of the free-market (or perhaps should be understood as the individual de-decommodifying the state's investment in education); it does however represent a shift away from being a citizen whose life is shaped by the framework of the welfare state.

In the UK, following the Second World War, a fundamental shift occurs in how British society is understood to organise itself. This materialises in the creation of a different welfare state, one that looks to remedy endemic social problems by greater state intervention. The invocation by Beveridge of squalor, ignorance, want, idleness and disease as the 'five Giant Evils' (Beveridge, 1943), in its very archaic language, suggested that change was long overdue. The consequent state interventions – National Insurance, the National Health Service and tripartite education system – reflect the start of a social process in which Beveridge's language would relentlessly (and rightly) change. Squalor and want would become understood in the nomenclature of poverty, homelessness and inequality; idleness as unemployment; disease as health etc. The shift in language reflects the sort of modernising society described by Beck (1992) in which both technological change is impacting upon industry and the economy and also 'the *sources of certainty* on which life feeds are changed' (Beck, 1992: 50, original emphasis). Such certainties might include lifestyle choices, identity politics, political participation and the distribution of power.

In the post-war landscape one potent account of the impact of modernising process at a societal level occurs in T.H. Marshall's description of citizenship (Marshall and Bottomore, 1992). Marshall outlines the rights and duties of citizens and in doing so notes that education is a duty of citizenship rather than a right resting with the individual. In this context, a twofold sense of risk emerges for home educators: on the one hand potential failures to acquire skills and knowledge and on the other a failure to become citizens. This wider failing is perhaps more regularly voiced in terms of home education failing to provide children with adequate socialisation, often described in very localised terms such as children not developing social skills based on interactions with other children. By making the decision to home educate their children, families do actively distance themselves from the state, community and society, which may be viewed as both undemocratic (Reich, 2005) and in large part, selfish (Apple, 2000; Lubienski, 2000). The decision to home educate consciously isolates families, including their children, who will not have the opportunity to socialise with those from different backgrounds to themselves (Apple, 2000; Evans, 2003; Reich, 2005). Such isolation may be understood in a wider context of inclusive and exclusive practices associated with being a citizen, in terms of the energies the state might expend to produce a functioning, cohesive society. Such a society may not necessarily present the most appealing vision: functioning and cohesive for example, could quickly become associated with being unchanging, over-bearing and restrictive.

Risk and changing economies

Beck identifies a period of time in which there has been a shift in organising social and political processes and a shift in how these processes are perceived. By locating his arguments within a specific time frame, he presents an identifiable account of late-capitalist society distinguished by recognisable characteristics, e.g. that it is a global society driven by information and technological networks. In other words it is distinct from an earlier historic period. Scott (2000) unpicks a range of dualisms deployed by Beck, including the shift from collectivisation and tradition as the fundamental organising principles of society to individualisation and reflexivity; how concerns about social justice and inequality determined by class and wealth have been superseded by concerns about exposure to risk; and, how traditional patterns of class consciousness have been eroded to be replaced with newer fears of risk and the need to reduce risk in order to promote both collective and individual security. It's a 'big picture' of the world and one that perhaps reflects a Western outlook that sees security at home threatened by unmanageable risks abroad, (e.g. global pollution or mass migration), or at the hands of natural disasters. Ironically it is a narrative that resonates in some part because it repeats, in a very broad brush fashion, the understandings of major catastrophic historical events: dinosaurs obliterated in a blink of the ice age or European populations decimated by the Black Death. The potential for extreme upheaval and change to secure communities is therefore understood as both a reality (a tsunami could happen today), and something evidenced epochally (the past was shaped by big events). It is necessarily a global conceptualisation of risk, though one understood at the personal, local level.

To engage with global shifts of economies and the means of production, of identities and risks, requires a shift in how the world is perceived by individuals characterised as being both reflexive and cosmopolitan; it 'demands a new

26 *Situating home education in global education*

outlook, from which we can grasp the social and political realities in which we live and act. Thus the cosmopolitan outlook is both the presupposition and the result of a conceptual configuration of our modes of perception' (Beck, 2006: 3). In this new cosmopolitan world, 'cultural ties, loyalties and identities have expanded beyond national borders and systems of control' (Beck, 2006: 7). Within education economies this might be seen in the development of transnational universities; global league tables; MOOCS (Massive Online Open Courses); and schooling perceived as the normative approach to education. An increase in homeschooling in Western developed nations potentially disrupts the shared perception of cosmopolitanism by looking inward and reflecting a turn back towards community and family. Such an account might reflect a fractured and troubled society in which we live; but in terms of practice, it could also provide evidence of individuals managing global risks in a potentially effective manner. In the case studies of home educators that follow there is an examination of how the perceptions of different home educators identify both some families as managing risk successfully and others as insular and disengaged with society. In this respect there appears a sense in which the moral panics that might emerge around certain groups of people based on characteristics such as social class, ethnicity or religion, feed into an argument that they are backward-looking and a threat. Meanwhile other families are identified as proactive, modern and addressing the hazards and opportunities in their lives.

The identification of some home educators as doing the best for their families whilst others are responsible for introducing risk poses interesting questions about how boundaries are being created. Whilst for Beck boundaries that once existed between the national and international are seen to dissipate because of the essential unmanageability of crises within national borders (e.g. pollution produced on one side of the world will impact on the other side); the perception of difference between different home educators generates newer boundaries. Such boundaries often seem to be shaped by very traditional allegiances. Gypsies for example have faced extraordinary histories of intolerance both globally and locally and this seems to be readily apparent in the creation of narratives that identify home education of Gypsy children as problematic and a risk (Bhopal and Myers, 2016). Ironically Gypsy families have traditionally used home education in the UK as a means of managing clearly defined risks faced by their communities. In many respects this can be quantified as having been a successful strategy, certainly in terms of protecting the communities' cultures and values. As a means of managing risk, Gypsies could be identified as a global migratory population who, over considerable periods of time, have managed and deployed their resources to ensure their survival in a global context. Such an account does not have widespread traction and in global terms they remain Bauman's 'have nots' – identified as unable to deploy wealth and privilege as effectively as global elites (Bauman, 2000). The historic patterns of such a global positioning can be clearly delineated and this suggests that old boundaries and old racisms are at work in how Gypsy home educators fit into a discourse about education (Myers, 2018). This may suggest that the power of the local to impact on a global conception of the world goes beyond Beck's suggestion that there is just a 'longing' for the 're-establishment of the old boundary lines' (2006: 8) marked by sentiments such as pity and hatred. Instead, old racisms are re-emerging to define new settings and the transparency of a boundary-less state is an illusory concept. For Wacquant this might reflect the work of the state, but it also appears to build on the deeply held stereotypes and racisms of citizens shaping the state in their own image.

Individualisation and home education

One consequence of globalisation shaped within risk society that might be readily identifiable within the lives of home educators is a process in which the loss of 'traditional support networks' such as family and neighbours more widely means they have to 'rely on themselves and their own individual (labour market) fate with all its attendant risks, opportunities, and contradictions' (Beck, 1992: 92). Such individualisation however appears in a variety of forms in the accounts given in this book. Disconnections with family based on patterns of migration and feelings that schools no longer reflected the values of local communities (often because schools are heavily engaged in neo-liberal approaches within free-market economies), all figured strongly in the lives of respondents. Delivering an effective education to children using the resources available to families was a recognisable narrative and one that highlighted awareness of the importance of education for all different types of respondent. For Beck the importance of education relates to the construction of individual reflexive identities suited to life in late modernity; an educated person 'incorporates reflexive knowledge of the conditions and prospects of modernity, and in this way becomes an agent of reflexive modernisation' (1992: 93). For home educators this often described more of the process of delivering an education rather than the anticipated outcome for their children.

For some parents, particularly those from religious backgrounds, home education appeared to be a strategy designed in many ways to shield their children from the dangers of everyday society. Such dangers might be identified as having moral, political or ideological overtones, but invariably families sought to increase a sense of a privatisation of their lives in which their children were distanced from such dangers specifically, but also more generally from society. In many ways this unpicks some of the ironies of globalised lives which are managed at very local or individual levels. Beck for example describes how the 'isolation of privatised lives, shielded against all the other privatised lives, can be shattered by social and political events and developments of the most heterogeneous kind. Accordingly, *temporary* coalitions between *different groups* and *different camps* are formed and dissolved, depending on the *particular issue* at stake and on the *particular situation*' (Beck, 1992: 100, original emphasis). One of the successes of home education advocacy groups in both the United States and UK has been their ability to mobilise a shared political activism rooted in the strength of individualised identities. Although this is often presented in terms

28 *Situating home education in global education*

of a David and Goliath scenario, that understates the strength and capability generated by networks of very effectively aligned people with widely shared beliefs. The pressure of dealing with identifiable risks in the lives of families including the inequitable distribution of educational opportunities contributes further to already existing processes of individualisation. For families unhappy at modernisation and for marginalised families for whom modernisation is an ongoing repetition of real and perceived discrimination, these are conditions 'which compel people – for the sake of their own material survival – to make themselves the centre of their own planning and conduct of life' (Beck, 1992: 88). In doing so the tendency is to align with social identities that reflect the immediate concerns of everyday life, to be engaged more actively but within a narrower group of people. Whilst a traditional response to failing schools might have been to challenge state policy by engaging in political or class-based protest; these seem less effective when neo-liberal policies driving school policies are broadly shared across all strata of political life. One alternative, home education, side-steps changing state education for everyone and instead looks to take responsibility at an individual or family level.

The importance of family and the significance of the home are discussed throughout the case studies. For many home educators the importance of the family appears almost in opposition to progress through modernity. The risk they identify is of traditional values being lost as families are becoming more ambiguously understood and juggling a constellation of competing demands around careers, education, parenting and household chores. Whilst Beck anticipates a 'negotiated family' emerging in which traditional roles are reshaped and amalgamated, one of the ironies is an emergence of such families as home educators that fit that mould but are often highly nostalgic for traditional, 'lost' values. Such families act as cosmopolitan citizens taking hold of the reins of individualised choices around their children's education, but within their narratives is a common thread of seeking to reintroduce a traditional conception of family life. This was an experience shared amongst Black, White and Gypsy families; by evangelical Christians and Muslims; and by poorer and more middle-class families. In some respects the 'risks' of risk society were often managed by a retreat to the traditional. A greater sense of self and of control over lives both anticipated and reflected processes of individualisation whilst simultaneously making stronger networks within faith groups, communities and self-help networks.

Individualisation and consumption

The rise in numbers of home educators should therefore be regarded both in terms of how families are responding to changing economic, social and political conditions, but also in terms of how society is being shaped by their practices. Apple suggests a relationship between education and democracy that has in some respects been exploited in order to promote individualised consumption of the resources allocated to education. He describes a redistribution of

Situating home education in global education   29

public resources in the United States away from marginalised groups towards more effectively organised communities including religious homeschoolers. Such exploitation of public funding raises 'serious questions about the drain on economic resources' (2000: 75) in a climate of widespread budget cuts and can be linked to increasingly inequitable stratification along class and racial lines. It also underpins a changing democratic process; homeschooling for many on the religious right is a materialisation of ideological beliefs that privilege a move towards 'private consciousness' and open hostility and fear of a 'managerial state' (Apple, 2005). Historically, in Rousseau's (1959) sense of the individual being more self-aware, individualisation may have prefigured a movement towards civic democracy and towards a dialogic self-awareness and engagement with others (Taylor and Gutmann, 1992).

The positioning of education, schooling and homeschooling within democratic understandings of the public and common good is highly contentious and exposes fault-lines in how individuals understand their relationship to their communities. In principle increasing the numbers of homeschoolers results in lower school rolls, with both savings made within education budgets, and also contributing to improving standards, if pressure on teaching staff and infrastructure is reduced (Hill, 2000). However as Apple notes, there is also evidence of a redistribution of funding towards homeschoolers and often this occurs in a very inequitable fashion. The immediate financial benefits may have other less welcome social consequences if fewer parents have a personal investment in the outcome of voting or other democratic change to address school quality or funding (Hill, 2000). So whilst an individual awareness of the 'cost' of education has substance and can be evidenced, it needs to be set against the 'value' of entering into democratic dialogues. Lubienski (2000) also makes a broader argument about homeschooling being detrimental to democratic citizenship because it results in the withdrawal of both economic and social capital from the public school system. School funds are adversely impacted by declining school rolls with state government's investing less not just in teaching but also less in the infrastructure of schools. More importantly public schools are founded on democratic principles that

> serve more than simply the individual private interests of their immediate users (students and their families). Thus governance and funding are shared throughout the community – by users and nonusers, future employers, parents, nonparents, future parents and parents whose children are no longer in school.
>
> (Lubienski, 2000: 211–212)

The withdrawal of pupils implicitly withdraws the engagement of those pupils, their families and their communities in processes to change or improve schools and as such, 'home schooling is not only a reaction to, but also a cause of declining public schools' (Lubienski, 2000: 207). With fewer interested parties scrutinising and engaged in the process of education funding, democratic

30 *Situating home education in global education*

processes that should ensure schools are required to improve are more likely to be side-lined. Citizenship rests upon a balance between rights and duties and homeschooling undermines the responsibilities or duties associated with being a citizen. Rather than working towards the 'public good', homeschoolers place greater value on a privatised set of individual or family rights.

Apple also suggests the individualisation that characterises homeschoolers is very different to that identified by Rousseau and reflects a process in which 'democracy has been reduced to consumption practices. Citizenship has been reduced to possessive individualism; and a politics of resentment and a fear of the 'other' has been pressed forward' (2005: 77). Individualisation materialises not as a means of asserting shared freedoms and engagement with different neighbours and communities but rather as something divisive. It is a process in which some communities disengage from others and do so as an effective economic strategy. It is also an effective political strategy in which the personal ideology 'of largely white working class and middle class groups that mistrust the state and are concerned with security, the family, gender and age relations within the home; sexuality and traditional and fundamentalist religious values and knowledge' (Apple, 2005: 78) converges with neo-liberal and neo-conservative politicians. Homeschoolers can express their individuality through the control they exercise over their children's education whilst benefiting economically and politically. They have both 'a new ability to personalise information, to choose what they want to know or what they find personally interesting' (Apple, 2005: 78); and, simultaneously to undermine the stability of other communities with whom they do not find common ground. In this way the democratic process shifts away from recognising a broad spectrum of society and privileges a substantial cohort of like-minded individualists.

The pattern of home educators successfully adopting strategies within neo-liberal policy making is also evident in the United Kingdom; Conroy argues that,

> Nowhere are the social anxieties and the effects of populism more evident than in recent British government responses to the growth of elective home education, and nowhere is the contest between parent and state more evident or more potentially inflammatory than in the domain of home education.
>
> (2010: 330)

British home educators however have been less successful in accessing a redistribution of resources. A common complaint from home educators is that local authorities largely relinquish any responsibility, including financial, for the support of home-educated children. Education funding is largely based on schools being funded on a per pupil basis. It is worth speculating however on the impact increasing marketization may have on the distribution of funding; the traditional arrangement of local authorities holding the purse strings for all the schools in their area is being progressively moved towards a model in which central government funds individual schools or networks of schools, often managed on a commercial basis. The freedoms this allows for schools to reimagine curriculums and pedagogic practice is only beginning to become fully understood. It is possible to envisage schools adapting in some respects to pedagogies supportive of home education practice in the future, in much the same way that Charter schools have done in order to engage with homeschoolers in the United States. Some evidence of how schools have adapted around policy is evident in the confusion that seemed to arise around children described as being home educated whilst attending unregistered faith schools (Myers and Bhopal, 2018). In these cases it was only the jockeying around nomenclature of being a home educator rather than access to state funding for schools that was at stake, but that may change in the future. There is the potential for neoliberal policy making in the United Kingdom to both privilege the individual's right to choose economic, social and cultural practices they believe in, whilst at the same time jeopardising economic and political security. Citizenship within a neo-liberal context may well change its meaning; Conroy (2010) suggests that whilst the state has responsibilities in relation to children's education and upbringing, 'they must make certain presumptions in favour of the parent if the government responses to home education are to be considered political rather than populist and controlling' (2010: 325). In many ways this underlines the shift in public perceptions since the extension of compulsory education in 1944 which was almost universally regarded as a positive intervention by the state within family life.

Schools and the 'other'

Home education is not a new phenomenon. If anything, the introduction of 'schooling' outside of the family is a more recent form of education. Baker and LeTendre (2005) note that 'mass schooling' is a revolutionary turn away from small-scale, local practices that existed within families and communities for centuries and typically ensured individuals learned a simple set of skills in order to survive within their communities. They also contend that in many ways the success of schools as a global homogenous practice goes unnoticed as individual states and regions tend to (mistakenly) identify their schools as representing unique and local institutions reflecting the specifics of their geographic entity. It is only within the last 200 years that the transition towards obligatory schooling has become part of children's experience. Whilst this may have begun in Western, developed nations, it rapidly becomes a ubiquitous feature of all countries. Similarly there has been a rapid movement from schooling solely for younger, primary school-aged children towards ensuring children attend secondary school. Whilst schooling itself has become a norm of global societies, Meyer (2001) discusses the continuing schism that has delineated how education is valued within societies. On the one hand, the state identifies its primacy in the role of maintaining and developing the identity and values of the citizen body; on the other hand, a more 'society-centered vision' (2001: 13) sees the state as just one amongst many institutions that needs to be regulated by society generally.

32 *Situating home education in global education*

Home educators sit interestingly within these historic transitions and wider debates about the role education should play in children's lives and society more generally. Supporters of home education have argued that in the past when home education was the norm it is easy to provide evidence that it was a successful strategy and that the introduction of schooling coincides with a decline in academic standards (Gaither, 2008). More contemporary research has also claimed home-educated children perform better than their school-attending peers (Rudner, 1999: Ray, 2013). Martin-Chang and Levesque (2016) note that too much research that purports to provide evidence of the academic successes of home education is flawed by being commissioned and conducted by home educators looking to promote their personal standpoints. Similar flaws in research methodologies are also highlighted by Neuman and Guterman (2016) and, perhaps more pertinently, they suggest that children in some settings do very well whilst others do not and that comparisons between home-educated and schooled children often attempt to compare essentially different outcomes and curricula. A body of evidence does emerge to suggest structured home education environments produce better academic results than schools but that unstructured environments are less successful (Martin-Chang et al., 2011; Neuman and Guterman, 2016).

The historic positioning of home education tends therefore to situate it as a practice prevalent in the past but superseded by schooling; as something small-scale and local rather than tied to national interests or global change; and, generally less academically successful when not mirroring standard school practice. As such, families choosing home education today are likely to be viewed as being in some respects backward-looking and attempting to recreate a historically redundant education. Such accounts might tap into sentimentality and a rose-tinted view of how life used to be framed within understandings of domesticity and the centrality of family life. The primacy of family responsibility for education amongst home educators in the United States is well documented but is less a feature of research in the United Kingdom. Some accounts of the emotional and affective lives of home educators begin to identify both the importance of the domesticity of the *home* space in home education and the relationship between home education practice and understandings of family life (Kraftl, 2013). For some home educators their decision represents a holistic engagement with the family – one that might be understood in terms of reconnecting with a simpler past or with a more 'natural' way of life (Neuman and Aviram, 2003).

Obviously home educators would rail against descriptions describing them as backward-looking or driven by sentimentality; and be more likely to situate their narratives within a 'society-centred' version and perhaps holding the state to some extent accountable for its failings. It is worth highlighting that the families interviewed in this research tended to identify a vast range of different experiences. Some clearly felt the state was intrusive and prone to assimilating and devouring their culture; others complained the state failed the needs of their children and that home education was 'the only choice' left to them

Situating home education in global education 33

and symptomatic of being excluded. The sense of being either assimilated or excluded perhaps hints at a shared 'otherness' that typified home-educating families; however different their individual circumstances were, they were identified by or situated within the school system as 'others'. Bauman (1997) notes the complementary nature of assimilatory and excluding strategies the state often deploys when its need for order and homogeneity encounters the disorder of the *stranger*. Some of these materialised in the approaches taken towards different families based on their personal characteristics.

Pattison (2015) notes how labels such as 'home education' and 'homeschool' challenges both widely-held understandings of the home and the school and the relationships that are presumed to exist between them. This resonates with Kraftl's discussion of the intimacy of the home but in a slightly unsettling fashion. Just as the *stranger* is often described in terms of the uncomfortable proximity of an unknown and distant figure, so to the proximity of the school, representative of the state within the home setting, 'physically disrupts the social rules of time and space, and conceptually disturbs the cultural and social binaries of home and school. It is an othered and othering space of society' (Pattison, 2015: 16). These othered relationships form the basis for the case studies in the remainder of this book. What often stands out however is not so much that being othered and different makes for difficult or contentious lives. Rather the vast majority of parents in our research appeared to lead remarkably ordinary lives. They were universally engaged and interested in their children's education and in the importance of doing what they could to guarantee the long-term security and lessening of risk in their family life. That said, many of them felt their experiences of schooling were a let-down; some experienced bullying or racism; other families identified failures to understand their personal circumstances or differences specific to their family; and some felt schools were not delivering the academic standards required. For most families there was not one single reason for becoming home educators. Their accounts are, for the most part, situated within recognitions of how individuals, families, communities and citizens interact together.

4 Middle-class families

'Our children do better at home'

One recurrent theme that emerges in both academic and non-academic accounts of home education is that it is a predominantly middle-class endeavour. There is evidence to suggest that home educators tend to be financially secure, from middle-class socio-economic backgrounds (Belfield, 2004) and have high levels of education (Sutton and Bogan, 2005). Such families are likely to cite falling academic standards in schools as a key reason why parents choose to home educate (McKeon, 2007), as well as the relevance of the curriculum taught in schools (Welner and Welner, 1999) and the perception of regimented structural organisation of schools and its impacts on pupil's learning (Arai, 2000). Often mothers are identified as being more likely than fathers to bear responsibility for home educating their children (Stevens, 2001). During our research, we spoke to a much broader section of home educators but we also interviewed many families who self-identified as being middle class and seemingly matched such characteristics.

This chapter will explore the experiences of middle-class families who have chosen home education for their children at primary school age. It will draw upon case studies with two home-educating families who define themselves as middle class. The decision to home educate at a younger age before children returned to state schooling for a secondary education was a commonplace approach adopted by a large number of respondents. In particular it was often a decision that was made by families who were dissatisfied with the quality of primary school education and/or families who felt that there was an emotional and social need to preserve the bonds between parents and children. Several parents described a desire to extend childhood. They suggested that the pressures of attending school foreclosed the innocence and playfulness of being a child, replacing it with the non-childlike pressures of tests, measurement and achievement. One irony perhaps was that these parents were typically parents who placed a high value on academic achievement (related to succeeding in the future), and who identified the value of attending 'good' secondary schools that were achieving higher GCSE and A Level results and demonstrating better university progression rates.

In our research, such families tended to identify as being middle class and often appeared to be relatively affluent; e.g. they were home-owners, both

Middle-class families   35

parents were in employment, often in professional jobs and in possession of skills and training that would facilitate a return to the labour market after taking a break to home educate in the short term. Often the decision to home educate seemed to reflect a choice that was available to the parents because they had options about how to deploy their economic capital. It was a choice that was predominantly exercised for younger children, generally those attending primary school. There is an interesting comparison to be made with families who used state schooling at an earlier age before withdrawing their children from secondary education. This includes Gypsy families who as their children become older often found schools less able to deliver their needs, and, families whose children have special educational needs associated with disabilities who found the further their children progressed in schooling, the harder it was for them to receive the education they wanted. These families often felt they had 'no choice' in the decisions they made to support their children; whereas more affluent families often spoke in terms of making the 'best choice' for their children and their family.

One finding that emerged from discussions with middle-class families was that they built a framework around their home education practice that seemed to encompass a wider sense of family identity. So for example, there were consistent accounts from many middle-class respondents about attending social functions with other home-educating parents, setting-up or attending self-help groups, or spending time socially with other parents. This suggested that parents 'bought in' not just to the value of home education for their children, but also, a social identity that merged the role of being a home-educating parent/family with other markers of identity. It can be argued that such an analysis applies in other contexts of home education (e.g. the evangelical Christian families discussed in Chapter 6). However, it often felt that middle-class home educators were specifically creating a world of like-minded, similarly affluent and economically situated families to mix with. By doing so, they provided a very safe environment for their children so that they only ever encountered other children just like themselves. They were not exposed to children from different social, economic or racial backgrounds for example (and again such comparisons can, and are, made about other groups who chose home education). Such decisions have a clear resonance with the reasons parents might choose private education in order to access or transfer social and cultural capital intergenerationally. More generally such educational processes can be understood in terms of the reproduction of class and social status (Bourdieu and Passeron, 1977). Many families stressed the value they placed upon their own abilities to produce the best results for their children. When allied to a limited mixing with like-minded, similarly classed other families, it would be hard to imagine such approaches producing identities other than homogenous reproductions of their parents and/or their parents' friends' children. The social element of these home educators is interesting in relation to the often-cited criticism of home education. Almost all the parents interviewed in this category of parents

36   *Middle-class families*

noted they created strong social settings in which their children could engage with other children and adults. The parents did not generally suggest they felt isolated or lonely; far from it, it was more common to hear about parents and children having fun, playing with friends and embarking on great adventures. The process of becoming a home educator in many respects was linked to a fully engaged social life.

The two case studies chosen for this chapter describe two typical examples of middle-class families interviewed in the research. The first is a family who was largely just dissatisfied with problems identified in their local schools' teaching practice; the second is perhaps a more complicated decision made by a family about meeting the wider needs of the family.

The Miltons

The Milton family live on the South Coast in a semi-rural village. The area in which the Miltons live is predominantly White and the village is situated within one of the safest Conservative seats in the country. The village is one of several villages that radiate from a nearby small commuter town served by fast trains into London and across the south-east. The village is considered comparatively wealthy and middle class compared to other nearby villages and its population is characterised as families from professional backgrounds often with young children and a sizeable proportion of retired people. There are several small pockets of ex-council housing on the outskirts of the village that has either been sold to owner-occupiers or to housing associations. Many houses in the village have posters expressing opposition to planned developments of new housing and infrastructure in the locality.

Mrs Milton has primary responsibility for all aspects of the family's domestic arrangements, including making all the important decisions around their children's upbringing. Mrs Milton was a well-spoken and articulate respondent who described both her family and herself as being middle class. Discussing her own background, Mrs Milton noted that she was 'educated' and had been to university. Going to university was characterised as being an important and exciting time in her life associated with moving away from her home (she had grown up in a town close to where she now lived), and going to live in London.

After university she worked as an administrator in local government until the birth of her first child, at which time she stopped being in paid employment. Recently she started her own business selling refurbished furniture and second-hand designer clothes on eBay and at car boot sales and markets. Mrs Milton explained,

> I was totally upfront with Ian (her husband). When we had children they would be my priority not him. He knows that and he knows what I'm like. He's very quiet so I make the decisions. As soon as I was pregnant I announced we would move here. And that's what we did. We set up shop in (village name) and we've been here ever since.

Mrs Milton's husband, Ian, also went to university before joining the merchant navy. He is now a Chief Officer and consequently is often away for long periods of time during the year. The Miltons have three daughters; Chloe aged 14, Emma aged 13 and Jess aged 10. Both of her older daughters attend the local comprehensive secondary school, but Mrs Milton home educates her youngest daughter Jess and has been doing so for two years. The Miltons also look after a large number of pets and animals including three dogs, several cats, a large reptile, an outdoor aviary, rabbits, hens and geese.

All of the Milton children attended their local primary school that was recently graded as 'outstanding' by OFSTED.[1] Chloe and Emma completed all their primary education in the school. Jess completed four years in the school until two years ago when Mrs Milton decided to educate her youngest daughter at home. It is a small school with one class intake of children a year and is a short walk away from the family home, next door to a village hall and park. Mrs Milton said she was pleased with her local primary school for a long time. Her husband spent long periods of time away from the family home working and she was often the one who made the day to day and major decisions to do with the children's education. For example, she was the one who attended parent evenings, school events and spoke to the teachers should any issues arise with the children. Mrs Milton described her reasons for home educating.

> I did like the school for a long time. Both of my oldest children attended the school for the whole of their primary schools and it was great. But then I noticed that some new teachers had joined the school and I wasn't very happy with the education that Jess was getting. Some of the teachers were just coming across as though they didn't really know how to teach and I didn't think Jess was getting much out of it so I decided to do it myself.

Mrs Milton felt that Jess was not particularly progressing in her reading, writing and speaking skills. When she asked the teacher about this, the teacher was unable to give a clear explanation as to why she was not progressing.

> I did speak to Jess's teacher several times and one parents' evening I really did wonder why this teacher was allowed to teach. She had not listened to Jess read for a whole term and did not even know what her progression levels were. When I asked her who her friends were she could not name any of them. At that point, I just thought that this was all a waste of time. She hadn't heard her read for the whole term and could not assess her progress or levels. That was when I decided that I could do this myself.

Mrs Milton described the decision-making processes she went through before taking Jess out of school. This happened in a relatively quick time frame ("weeks rather than months"). In particular she researched homeschooling online. She was surprised by the apparently large numbers of families home educating and also by how positive other family's experiences were. She also

38 *Middle-class families*

spoke to a number of parents at the school including those with experience of education such as teachers and university lecturers. She finally made the decision, but without consulting her husband who was working outside of the country at the time,

> I didn't just take Jess out of school, I asked a few parents who are teachers what their views were about home education. They were quite mixed to be honest, some said it was a good thing especially as many teachers did not invest so much in their pupil's education – certainly not as much as parents would – others said that it was easier to send them to school and was stressful if you have to do it yourself.

Mrs Milton was keen to discuss what she felt education meant for her. She did not necessarily feel or think that children attending primary school was just about academic learning.

> I think there are many ways in which you can educate your children. They don't have to be in a classroom all day sitting on chairs and listening to what usually is very structured and does not engage them. It can be about different things, they can go to museums, to the beach, to the woods and experience different things – this is still an education for them. I also want my children to build friendships. Not necessarily that will last forever, but just develop all the skills they will need in the future to talk to people and build relationships.

Mrs Milton spoke about the reaction that she received from the school when she told them she had decided she was going to home educate.

> It was interesting because none of the teachers questioned that I would be capable of educating Jess, they were more concerned that I would be isolated and Jess would be on her own. But that hasn't happened at all to us. I have met people by going out and met families who are not at school when we have gone out. This way we have been able to support each other. I was going to join organisations but found that meeting people when I was out was fine. And I've always been sociable; I think I know everyone in about a ten mile radius.

Mrs Milton mentioned that she had been in touch briefly with 'Education Otherwise', an independent organisation in England that provides support for home educating parents including curriculum material, legal advice and access to support networks. Unlike many other parents we interviewed, Mrs Milton used this organisation primarily as a means of gathering information and advice rather than to access other similar families. She described her own extensive social networks of friends, often other mothers whose children had attended

Middle-class families   39

the same primary school, and how these networks formed the basis of her daily routines. One criticism Mrs Milton made of the school was its regimented nature and strict rules which she felt did not suit Jess;

> One of the key things that is very useful for us, mainly for Jess is that the day is not structured and the days are not the same. We can do what we want, when we want. Sometimes we might stay at home and read and play. Other times we may go out and visit an art gallery or a museum. We walk Derek and Mary's (elderly neighbours) dogs most days and I might arrange to meet up with a girlfriend for coffee. Having the options to do this is really beneficial and I think the whole experience is more enjoyable for Jess. She doesn't have to sit at her desk worrying she's got a maths test to pass.

Mrs Milton also described a strong set of bonds between Jess and her two elder siblings. She placed a great deal of emphasis on joint activities that brought the four of them together including social activities and also their busy domestic arrangements such as looking after their small menagerie. Within these discussions the one figure who was noticeably absent was Mr Milton. He was abroad during the research but reflected on the decision to home educate during a number of skype interviews. Mr Milton confirmed he had no say in the decision, but that he trusted his wife's 'instincts' about their children's welfare. All these conversations were conducted with Mrs Milton fully engaged in the conversation. Mr Milton noted that he was surprised that his wife had made the decision, but pointed out that in respect of his wife, 'everything moves very quickly, when she makes a decision she gets on with it'. Mr Milton also felt that the children would not be disadvantaged socially, noting that the family, (particularly through his wife), had a busy social life and that the 'girls' always did lots of things together. It did feel as though the Miltons lived parallel lives: he away from home and distanced from all the domestic arrangements, whilst she was actively filling her life with social activities and motherhood. When asked specifically if her husband's long absences from home had a bearing on her decision to home educate, Mrs Milton suggested this had crossed her mind. She described quite candidly how the decision to take her youngest daughter out of school was one way of extending her role as a mother and primary caregiver. However, she also pointed out that, in some respects against her husband's wishes, she had begun to seek out opportunities to earn money buying and selling vintage clothing. She described this as part of the process of seeing her children grow up and her parenting role diminish. She also noted,

> We are very close. The girls and me. And I don't think that will ever change. It's better that Jess is at home now but in two years she will go back to school. I think it's just about getting through a difficult patch with the school. I do love it though.

40 *Middle-class families*

Mrs Milton also felt that the school's emphasis on testing children and preparing them for SATs[2] put a great deal of pressure on children, something that home-educated children did not have to think about. The school that Jess had attended was graded as 'outstanding' for many years and there was a great deal of pressure for the school to maintain this reputation and to keep its high standards. This pressure was often transferred onto the children and their parents.

> One of the things that also made me want to home educate Jess was the pressure that there was on her to do well for her SATs. The school is very good, but the teachers put a lot of pressure on the children to do well. There are expectations that are too high for many of the children and so if they don't do well, then they might be labelled as not being very academic or very clever. I am glad that I took Jess out of that situation because now I know she is more relaxed and does not feel pressured by anything.

Since taking Jess out of school, Mrs Milton described how she had reflected upon her role as a home educator. She wished she had the confidence to do so earlier,

> I was scared when I made the decision to take Jess out of school. But now that I have been doing it for a few years, it's really not that hard. I think I am doing a better job than the teachers. Even though I am not a teacher I have a degree and I am not stupid and I also know the kinds of things that Jess should be doing and should be able to do at her age. In hindsight, I do feel that I wish I had the confidence to have home educated my older two at home. They would have been more happier and less pressured I think.

Despite her confidence that home education was the right decision for Jess, Mrs Milton also described how she felt under pressure to ensure that Jess did well and was able to read, write and do other things that Jess's peers were able to do.

> Jess is still very close friends with girls who are not home educated and sometimes I feel under a lot of pressure to ensure that Jess is in some ways like them and able to do the things that they are doing. It can be isolating for me, because sometimes it is hard to admit that you are under pressure to others. Some of the parents also question me and judge me because not all of them think that home education is a good idea for all sorts of reasons.

Mrs Milton spoke about some discussions she had with parents who indicated that she was in fact disadvantaging Jess, and was being selfish to have taken the decision to home educate.

> I don't know why some parents feel they think that it's ok for them to judge you. Some mothers have said that I am being very selfish taking

Jess out of school, they have almost compared to it abuse in some way. They think that Jess will be very disadvantaged because she is not going to school, and it is only something that benefits me. I think it is interesting that parents would rather send their children to school with a bad teacher rather than thinking that itself is a waste of time.

In other instances, Mrs Milton spoke about how she was seen as someone who was well qualified to educate their child at home, something that she attributed to social class. She consciously described class in terms of attributes such as being articulate and in relation to wider social skills that might sit within definitions of social capital. A recurring theme in Mrs Milton's description of her daily life, was of embarking on an outing with Jess and encountering an interesting person and having a conversation with them. Invariably the person described would have the attributes of being middle-class and educated. These encounters tended to suggest a reinforcement of Mrs Milton's own middle-class, affluent, educated and capable home educator identity.

> When I take Jess to the library – which we do every week and to the gallery which we also do regularly – I often end up speaking to lots of different people. It's very interesting how people judge you and react to you when you say you are home educating. I think it is class related, many people assume I must have been a teacher and so am able to do this. But I think others, who may not come across perhaps in the ways that I do, may be judged harshly and not seen as being able to take on that role. It could be that home education is seen more as something that middle class families are more willing to do than working class families. In all honesty, that has been my experience. All of the families that I have met have been very middle class and some have been ex-teachers.

When asked how she felt about parents who were perhaps less educated themselves choosing home education, Mrs Milton was clear they needed to be able to demonstrate some capability to educate their children. She related this to 'class' and 'level of education' in particular, but recognised, 'it's a free country'. She said how surprised she was that there was no monitoring of what she was doing with her children and again came back to the phrase 'it's a free country'. Mr Milton also mentioned how he had been worried there might be repercussions on the family if they were ineffective as home educators and noted how surprised he was that no one monitored their decision.

When asked whether the family would consider continuing to home educate Jess when she was secondary school age, Mrs Milton was very clear this was not an option,

> I have considered whether I would want to continue to home educate Jess when she turned 12 but I think at that age it might be better for her to go to secondary school. There are other issues that come to the fore then, she

42 Middle-class families

may want to be engaging and socialising with other girls her age and she will need to be thinking about what kind of subjects she wants to pursue in the future. I don't think I could prepare her for her GCSEs[3] and I think at that age she will probably want to be and should be socialising with girls her own age.

Mrs Milton was clearly aware of the different issues associated with home educating her child. She made the decision to do so based on the quality of education Jess was receiving from her teacher at the time. She felt that it was the right decision to make and also spoke about some of the pressures associated with being a home-educating parent. These included ensuring that Jess was at the same or similar educational levels as her friends such as being able to read, as well as being able to write about and engage in subjects such as Maths, History and Geography. Mrs Milton also spoke about how she and her daughter were judged by other families for her decision to home educate. This consisted of contrasting views; with some parents indicating she was being selfish and indeed comparing it to abuse and others who simply judged her in terms of her middle-class background and as someone who was competent and capable of home educating. Either way, Mrs Milton felt she had made the right decision but did not want to continue to home educate Jess as she approached secondary school age. Mrs Milton felt at this time she would resort back to formal schooling where Jess needed to be with her peers and have a more structured form of learning which would prepare her for her public GCSE exams. In hindsight, Mrs Milton indicated that she would have preferred to have educated her older two daughters at home during their primary school years. This perhaps suggests that her argument that the decision was just a temporary response to problems at the school masks her own pleasure at extending her role in the life of her younger daughter. Throughout Mrs Milton's account, there were continual references to her own management of her identity. This was closely aligned to her understanding of her daughter acquiring sets of skills and capabilities that reflected Mrs Milton's self-perception of herself as responsible, affluent and middle-class. Mrs Milton was clearly a sociable and engaging character and she was also very self-aware about her personality traits. She identified these aspects of her personality as being useful traits that it was worth passing on to her daughter.

One surprising finding was the speed and decisiveness with which Mrs Milton made the decision on behalf of her family (including Mr Milton). Although Mrs Milton described what she felt was a detailed and lengthy investigation of the options around home education, the feeling that the decision was actually made within one or two weeks and implemented within another two or three weeks feels remarkably quick. This speed was not reflected in other respondents who often described taking a long time to reach a decision, (the exceptions generally being some parents who were faced with more pressing or difficult problems at school e.g. encountering racism or bullying). The speedy action was also related to the subsequent ease with which Mrs Milton implemented home education; it felt as though within a short space of time this decision became a simple and easy part of her daily life. In many ways this reflected Mr Milton's observation that 'when (Mrs Milton) gets an idea in her head, it happens. Like that!'

The Stewarts

The Stewart family live in the south-easterly suburbs of London in a recognisably distinct, medium-sized town. They live within walking distance of a range of local services including shops and supermarkets, a library, a cinema, a municipal swimming pool and leisure complex. In addition there are regular, fast train services into central London. The town is associated with movement away from London to relatively cheaper housing in less densely populated areas; however this popular image hides a more complex and diverse social make-up. Different neighbourhoods are often distinguishable around particular types of housing including privately owned streets comprising of mostly terraced Victorian and Edwardian flats and houses; a large number of roads typified by privately owned 1950s suburban housing; post-war social housing much of which is now also privately owned; poorer social housing on estates built in the 1970s and 1980s; and, newer mixed developments. The Stewarts own a 1950s three-bedroomed house which they have extended by a loft conversion to provide two additional bedrooms. The street they live on is characterised as being relatively quiet and leafy. It is situated in a postcode that is considered to have added value to a lesser extent because of its close proximity to well-regarded primary schools, but more significantly because it almost guarantees places in a very successful secondary school. The Stewarts moved to this postcode with a specific intention of ensuring their children attended this particular school.

The Stewarts have three children, one boy and two girls. Julie is 15, Anna is 8 and Jack is 7. The Stewarts adopted Anna and Jack, who are biological siblings, five years previously when Mrs Stewart found out that due to medical complications having a second child would put her health in danger. Mr Stewart is a secondary school physics teacher and Mrs Stewart worked as a speech therapist until she gave up her job to educate Anna and Jack at home. Both Stewarts described themselves as a middle-class family; they own their own home and describe their financial situation as 'comfortable with little worries'. Initially Mr and Mrs Stewart disagreed about home educating their children, Mr Stewart was not convinced it was a good idea, but Mrs Stewart was adamant. The family had been home educating for a year.

> At first John (Mr Stewart) did not want me to take Anna and Jack out of school to educate them at home. He felt it would be too isolating for them and thought that if they were at school they could mix with other children and have the social aspect of learning as well. But to me, I thought that would have been too hard for them because they had a hard time before we adopted them.

44 Middle-class families

Mr Stewart voiced some concerns that he still felt about the decision to home educate;

> My day job is a teacher. And I'm committed to that. I would never work in a private school. I see the consequences of high-end education because my school is full of teachers who really care about everything we do. So I feel I might be letting my children down. Obviously we give them a great education at home, but some days I have doubts whether we are making the best choice.

Anna and Jack had experienced difficulties when they lived at home with their birth mother and due to periods of neglect, the children were taken into care at an early age. The Stewarts had adopted the children when they were 3 and 2 years old. According to Mrs Stewart,

> We had opposite views to be honest, John felt that the children would learn better at school and mix with others. I felt the complete opposite, I felt that the children didn't need to be with others and would find it very hard to mix with them given some of the issues they had in their lives. So I felt the best place for them was to stay at home.

Having jointly made the final decision to home educate their children, Mrs Stewart gave up her job to manage the daily routines this entailed.

> I was in a difficult position because I wanted to home educate and knew the only way that I could do this was to give up my job. I went to university and trained as a speech therapist and love my job but I just felt home education was the best choice for the children. At first I wasn't very confident but because John is a teacher it was easy as I could ask him lots of questions and that helps, but there is still conflict there because he thinks the children should be going to school. We have made a compromise though, we have agreed that they will be going to school when they are secondary school age.

Once Mrs Stewart had made the decision that she was going to home educate, she investigated different types of support she could access and what that support entailed. The greatest and most beneficial support she received was from other parents who were home educating and organisations that specialised in home education, which she found via other parents and the internet. However, she did not feel she received valuable support from the local authority.

> When I told the school that I was going to home educate my children, they didn't know how to deal with it at first because there aren't that many people who home educate that they know of. I think they said that I should contact the local authority to let them know and to see what kind of

support I could get. I did contact the local authority and again they didn't really have that much information on it. They told me what they could provide me with, which wasn't that much and then put me in touch with organisations which specialised in home education.

Mrs Stewart carried out a great deal of research and contacted various local home education organisations which provided her with a great deal of support. The support included curriculum materials, guidelines on legal issues regarding home education and how to contact other local parents who are home educating.

One particular organisation that I contacted was extremely useful, they gave me lots of excellent advice and guidance, things that I didn't get from my local authority which I should have got. I rely very much on the organisation because they have lots of different types of support that I can use and I can contact them anytime. The best support is the different resources they can provide and the learning materials I can use with the children.

Mrs Stewart mentioned that she felt she shared a lot in common with other home-educating parents she came into contact with.

Lots of the parents who I meet who are home educating come from similar backgrounds to me. They have all been to university and most of them were in professional jobs before they had their children. Most of them tend to be women, though not all. I do feel that home education attracts a certain kind of parent from a certain kind of background. That tends to be more middle class and professional and highly educated. Some of the parents were also teachers, if they have decided to home educate as well that is very interesting.

However Mr Stewart described other home-educating parents slightly differently,

They are the sort of parents I see at school who always think their child is suffering. Or their child isn't doing as well as they're capable of. Or their child is being picked on by the teacher. They're a type. The parents. They think their child is the centre of the stage.

When pushed on what sort of defining characteristics Mr Stewart might identify with home-educating parents, he suggested these would include 'middle-class', 'over-protective' and 'very, very self-confident'. Being 'self-confident' was a trait he identified from encountering other home educators at self-help groups. Mr Stewart suggested they were typically parents who were very convinced that their own choices were superior to all other options, even when faced by professional judgements suggesting otherwise. However when asked

46 Middle-class families

whether he felt this had a negative impact on home-educated children generally or his own children in particular, he suggested:

> It probably makes very little difference. Most of these kids are going to do well. It's like I said they're a type. If their kids were at school their mummies would be begging for them to be on a gifted and talented scheme or they would be getting private tuition from the head of maths. They're primed to do well. And the same happens if they're educated at home. These parents will make sure they get what they need. My two will be ok as well. They'll start secondary school in a few years and we'll talk to the teachers and they'll get all the support they need.

Mrs Stewart decided to home educate for various reasons, the main reason being that she felt very protective towards her children and because they had some difficult experiences she wanted to nurture them at home. She also felt that being educated did not necessarily entail going to school.

> The main reason I wanted to home educate the children was because they had been through such a hard time that I just wanted them at home with me. Another reason for me was that I don't believe that education is something that just has to take place in schools. We can educate our children in different ways by talking to them, introducing them to different things and also taking them out. I think as well that sometimes for children to not do anything is a good way for them to explore and think about things that interest them – rather than things being imposed upon them. Schools are very much about academic achievement and success, but education is not, it is much more than that.

The Stewarts were also fortunate in the help they received from Mrs Stewart's parents. They were both retired, lived locally and were very supportive of the family's decision in practical ways. This included regular babysitting and sometimes doing the family shopping. They also looked after the children every Tuesday to give Mrs Stewart a break.

> I am very lucky as I have my parents who have always supported me. When Julie was little they would always come and give me a break. Now they have Anna and Jack every Tuesday and look after them all day to give me a break. They can take them out or stay with them at their home, I don't mind what they do. It means the children get to spend time in a different environment with their grandparents and my parents really enjoy it too. But it also means that I have a break, a whole day to focus on something else which keeps me sane and enables me to think about other things. It is very refreshing for me.

Mrs Stewart described how her Tuesday had become her 'golden hour', with much of the day spent on going to the gym and meeting socially. Often these social arrangements took place with other home-educating parents that Mrs Stewart now knew as friends. In some respects this seemed to highlight that Mrs Stewart's involvement with home education went beyond just her engagement with the alternative schooling of her children and extended into a wide range of social practices. Mrs Stewart discussed some plans she had to start her own business; originally she intended using her training as a speech therapist as the basis for employment. However, she was now considering business models that might provide support to other home-educating parents. Despite suggesting that home educating her children was an at times overwhelming proposition, (and hence the need for wider family support), the engagement with other parents, (mothers in particular), was clearly very important to her above and beyond acting as a support mechanism because she was a home educator.

> I have other things that I need to do that help me to feel positive when I am at home with the children. Having one day in the week is good, because I don't have a weekend I am with the children all the time and a break is good for me. It means that I can go to the gym, meet some mums, have a chat. All that stuff you miss if you're not at work. That's why I wanted to start the business. I'm trying to find a little niche and I love being around with the mums, it's an ideal place for me.

When pressed on why she found the idea of starting a business supporting home-educating parents so attractive, Mrs Stewart returned to describing her relationships with other mothers in particular and commented they were "just like me". This perhaps echoed Mr Stewart's observation that home educating parents were a "type". When quizzed about other 'types' of home educating parents, (e.g. Gypsy families who traditionally home educated or parents whose children had disabilities), Mrs Stewart distinguished her position in relation to such parents. Specifically she felt that Gypsy parents probably made different choices about why they were home educating and families with disabled children would probably need to seek specialist provision that related directly to their individual circumstances. The types of families she identified for her business model, and which she openly equated to families with 'some spare cash kicking around', were middle-class families looking to have a break from home educating seven days a week, whose children would benefit from educational experiences. Mrs Stewart described how she prepared in detail for a visit to a local museum in order to make the visit, 'an experience' for her children. She felt it would be possible to replicate such practice for other home-educated children.

Looking to the future Mrs Stewart felt that home educating her two children was something she would not continue when they started secondary school.

> I agree with John – who firmly believes this – that the children should go to school when they start secondary school. By then, they will have more confidence and feel that they can go out in the big world and be able to

48   *Middle-class families*

cope. Also when they start secondary school, there are other skills they will need to learn. Such as how to interact with others, how to stick to a routine and how to have a structured timetable. This will help them to prepare for the real world and also to have friends who are the same age as them. I would like them to be able to take exams, do well and then go on to university. So for these reasons they will have to go to secondary school.

Mrs Stewart's expectations that her children would succeed in a more formal fashion at secondary school and university, seemed at odds with her holistic view of the distinctions between education and schooling. She placed a great deal of importance on education practices that went beyond formal, structured schooling; but this seemed to be associated specifically around younger, (i.e. primary school aged), rather than older experiences of education.

I think having an education is not the same as going to school. Going to school is formalised and is based on what is expected by the government for what our children should be doing. They also start school too early, in many other places they don't start until they are older. Getting an education isn't about sitting down and being told when to do things, what to do. It's more than that, it's about allowing children to have the freedom to be able to express themselves and to be children. School is about testing children so that they cannot concentrate on other things. There is too much pressure for young children today to do well. I didn't want my children to have that pressure, they have also had to contend with other things in their lives so don't need this kind of pressure.

Although the Stewart's decision to home educate was partly based on the quality of education her children were receiving at school, this was shaped by a sense in which the school was not positioned to provide for their children's personal and specific needs. The children had suffered problems during the early parts of their childhood and as a result were taken into care. Consequently, Mrs Stewart wanted to keep them with her in order that she could build their confidence and make them feel secure once they started secondary school.

Although the concerns around her children's well-being were clearly the focus for the decision to home educate, they sat within a constellation of competing demands about what was considered best for the children. These included Mrs Stewart's view that education did not directly equate to school attendance in which children were confined to classrooms with strict set of rules to be followed. She placed greater emphasis on children experiencing a variety of educational settings including visits to libraries, art galleries and museums; and also, being having greater independence and freedom to pursue their own interests. Like many parents (Arora, 2003), she was also concerned with the level of testing that pupils in primary schools were now subjected to and the additional pressures this brought to bear on her children. Mrs Stewart was adamant that at primary school age, children did not need to be tested constantly but needed to enjoy their early years by playing and being able to develop creatively as well as intellectually. She was also very well-informed through her involvement with home education organisations that some academic research has questioned the validity of testing by the state of children (Hardenbergh, 2015). Whilst Mr Stewart expressed some sympathy towards the view that unnecessary pressure was placed on children at too young an age, he appeared more pragmatic about how detrimental it might be to the child's overall development and was very clear that the children needed to attend secondary school in order to succeed in later life. As a family there was a definite understanding that all the Stewart children would attend secondary school. It was also hard not to conclude that Mrs Stewart found personal satisfaction in the process of being identified as a home-educating parent and that this was being channelled into her plans for a business. To a certain extent the current arrangements of the children not attending primary school but with a view to their returning to secondary school, the social world inhabited (primarily) by Mrs Stewart and her plans to start a business within this social world suggested the family had achieved a certain equilibrium balancing a number of competing demands. At the centre of this equilibrium was the identification of the adopted children's specific needs, but specific needs channelled through a family identity.

Conclusions

There are various reasons why families make the decision to home educate their children. Whilst some middle-class families identify specific problems such as bullying or alienation at primary schools as a trigger for taking their child out of school, most of the middle-class families we spoke to described experiences that closely mirrored those of the Stewart and Milton families. Such families tended to identify either generic failings in their local school and/or the more specific needs of their children. Relative affluence often made it easier to deploy a range of capitals (economic, social and cultural), in order to manage their children's education within a wider range of options than just sending their children to school.

Generally these decisions are not taken lightly. Parents conducted research on what home education involves; they tended to inform local authorities of their decision; and also generally contacted home education organisations to access support. Even Mrs Milton who appeared to unilaterally decide on her family's behalf in a short period of time that home education was the best choice, still went through a rigorous period of researching the implications of her decision. Many of the middle-class home educators stressed the hard work involved in their decision and how time consuming it could be. Some parents highlighted that it was often difficult to have a break from their children and this can be a cause of stress and anxiety. Few parents were as fortunate as Mrs Stewart, who was able to have a break once a week to pursue their own interests. However, despite identifying such problematic areas, there was still an overwhelming

50 *Middle-class families*

impression that for the parents who were directly involved in the home education of their children, this was considered a good choice. Not only did they identify the educational advantages for their children, but more widely there was a sense of parents engaged in routines that they enjoyed and appeared to thrive upon. In many respects this was an experience that was shaped both by affluence and by social behaviours. On the one hand, many of these families were well positioned financially to make choices that were not available to families reliant on two incomes. And, on the other hand, they were able to create a family identity in which the children's needs were reflected positively in daily parental behaviours; that is to say, the sort of social lives parents wanted to live were shaped to reflect the very positive accounts of how they actually lived. Balancing risk and choices in family life was reconciled in an equation in which the risks faced by their children were overcome by leading lifestyles they would choose to live regardless of having children.

Mr Stewart's observation that despite his misgivings about home education he did not anticipate it would impact negatively on his own children seemed quite telling. Both families identified the transfer of useful forms of social and cultural capital to their children. This happened directly in accounts of parents passing on specific social skills or of cultural knowledge acquired through visits to museums and galleries. It also happened in a more indirect fashion in the shaping of family identities that 'belonged' within networks of similarly affluent, successful families. There was little sense of children 'missing out' or being 'left behind'; middle-class parents seemed adept at putting in place strategies to ensure the long-term security of their children. The transmission of social and cultural capitals was entrenched in the teaching of skills and embodied behaviours (Bourdieu, 1977; Bourdieu and Passeron, 1977) that would ensure a smooth transition back to schooling. Such strategies were not the only option open to these families; they could as easily consider private schooling or move home to live within the catchment areas of better schools. Home education was just one amongst a number of similar strategies in which families deployed their resources to lessen potential risks (Beck, 1992, 2006) in their children's lives.

Notes

1 The Office for Standards in Education, Children's Services and Skills is an independent and impartial body which reports directly to parliament in England. It regularly inspects schools awarding them classifications of 'outstanding', 'good', 'requires improvement' and 'inadequate'.
2 Standardised Assessment Tests (SATs) take place in English primary schools at Key Stage 1 (age 7) and Key Stage 2 (age 11).
3 General Certificate of Secondary Education (GCSE) are exams taken at age 16 for pupils attending schools in England.

5 Gypsies and Travellers

'We have always educated our children at home'

This chapter focuses on the experiences of Gypsy and Traveller families who choose home education and specifically examines the experiences of such families in relation to the cultural norms and values of Gypsy and Traveller communities. It explores the discourses through which home education is negotiated in relation to traditional forms of schooling, and in turn how Gypsies and Travellers are positioned as marginalised groups within the context of education.

Many Gypsy families choose home education for many diverse reasons often depending on personal circumstances (D'Arcy, 2014; Myers and Bhopal, 2009). One clear distinction to emerge was a difference between families pursuing home education because it represented a traditional pathway that had historically been adopted within the family, whilst other families felt they were pushed into using home education because of failings in state education. One backdrop to such choices being made has been the well-documented increase in school attendance since the 1960s, driven in part by the need for Gypsies to adapt economically and acquire new skills from outside the community (Myers et al., 2010). These changes are often tempered by more traditional fears that materialise around adolescence about loss of identity, cultural appropriation and early-onset adulthood. As a result many Gypsy students attend primary school but fail to make the transition to secondary school or only spend a brief time at secondary school (Bhopal, 2004; Derrington, 2007; Myers et al., 2010). More generally, accessing schools is often made more difficult by wider problems encountered by Gypsy families including many problems in securing permanent accommodation (Myers, 2018; Vanderbeck, 2005). Other concerns about schooling voiced by parents in this research reflected widely documented difficulties faced by Gypsies including poor parental memories of their own schooling (Derrington and Kendall, 2008; Levinson, 2015) and fears of cultural assimilation and a lack of understanding for Gypsy culture (D'Arcy, 2017; Derrington and Kendall, 2008; Wilkin et al., 2010).

The case studies which follow explore the competing factors that affected two families. Significantly, despite leading very different lifestyles, both families were to some extent pushed towards adopting home education as their preferred educational route. The case studies raise two important issues. Firstly,

52 *Gypsies and Travellers*

they highlight systemic, structural racism in which the 'choices' available to some families are often very limited (Wilkin et al., 2010; Vanderbeck, 2005). In some respects there is evidence to suggest that schools simply reinforce deep-rooted societal inequalities. Secondly, there are clear concerns that poorer families are unable to access educational provision of an adequate standard for their children.

The Green family

Mr and Mrs Green describe themselves as English Gypsies. They have one 14-year-old daughter Amy who has been home educated for nearly three years since the age of 12. They live on a site on land that has been owned by their family for many years and is accessed by a private road. Their site is located on the outskirts of two small villages in a rural part of Sussex and the nearest town with significant shopping and leisure facilities is about 5 miles away.

The family live in a large (mobile) caravan within a discretely maintained plot of land that also encloses a workshop, some sheds and another fixed trailer. Other members of the Greens' extended family live on another plot of land within the site; these include Mr Green's brother and his family, Mr Green's uncle and his family and Mrs Green's mother. The extended family members live in fixed trailers all of which are situated within clearly demarcated plots of land. Mr Green owns two adjoining fields and these back on to a large nursery-holding. The overall impression from visiting the site on multiple occasions was that all the families enjoyed and relished living in a quiet and peaceful rural area. During the day the site was often deserted with only Mrs Green's mother at home. Describing relations between his extended family, Mr Green said, 'we are close and we stick together. Look after each other. But we all do our own thing. Nobody's sat in someone else's pocket'.

Mr Green described himself as an antiques dealer and owned a large warehouse, open to public and trade customers, which he sublet to a number of smaller antiques dealers. He highlighted his involvement in a variety of other business enterprises and in the past he had run various businesses including a garage and a building firm. The premises and motor mechanic business had been sold, but he maintained a particular interest in refurbishing classic cars. His family were well known in the local area both within Gypsy communities as a successful family and more widely because of his business interests. He was affluent and comfortable, owned several cars and a number of commercial properties.

Mrs Green described herself as a 'proper Gypsy. Born in a field.' When describing her role within the family, she explained that she adopted the 'traditional' roles for Gypsy women of managing all the domestic arrangements (e.g. childcare, housework), whilst her husband went out to work. In many respects this was not borne out during the research. Mrs Green was seen to take a great deal of hands-on interest in the management of the antiques warehouse and most of the interviews we conducted with her took place in her office at the warehouse. Mr Green had a separate office-cum-workshop at the warehouse. However, his daily work often appeared to be conducted away from the warehouse buying and selling antiques, whilst Mrs Green was responsible for managing relationships with the other dealers. The Greens had one daughter, Amy, who was fourteen. In the past Amy attended her local state primary school. She then spent 'about six weeks' at a nearby independent school but was withdrawn from that school in year 7 to be home educated.

The Greens felt it was very important for Amy to be educated to the highest level possible and accordingly they had prioritised their family arrangements to ensure she received such an education. Early in our interviews both parents identified non-traditional perspectives on gender roles by suggesting that Amy would need an education in order to get a job in the future and be able to support herself and not rely on a man to provide for her. Mr Green described how education had been an important aspect of Amy's life from a young age,

> We made sure that Amy went to school when she was in primary. It was really important that she was able to read and write and she needs to know how to do these things so that she can get a job. She needs qualifications now. Every job she wants will need qualifications. We want her to do well and get a job and so she had to go to school.

Both Mr and Mrs Green distinguished their approach to their child's upbringing from that of other Gypsy parents. They characterised some parents as being less concerned about girls securing an education, preferring they should stay at home, get married and take on the traditional Gypsy roles of wife and mother. According to Mrs Green,

> It's a laugh. They all moan their old man is useless and skint but they want to do the same thing for their kids. I wouldn't take it. (Mr Green), he brings home the bacon. He's a grafter. But I wouldn't want Amy relying on marrying someone like her dad. She's bright enough to do well on her own.

And Mr Green confirmed similar feelings,

> I won't comment on other people. They can do what they want. But I say to Amy you have to look after yourself. Don't rely on someone else doing for you what you can do yourself. You look at us – your mum and me – we've had ups and down but we always support ourselves. We never rely on other people.

There is a tradition of gender roles being divided in Gypsy and Traveller communities around adolescence, in which boys are expected to follow in their father's footsteps and help out in the family business; whilst girls become home makers before getting married at an early age (D'Arcy, 2014; Bhopal and Myers, 2008). The Greens clearly acknowledged a break from traditional Gypsy gender

54 *Gypsies and Travellers*

roles, whilst at the same time reiterating traditional sentiments about Amy being independent and self-supporting. Just as the distinction between gender roles was less traditional, so too was the identification of possible future job opportunities requiring qualifications; a more traditional path might have involved Amy taking greater responsibilities within the existing family businesses. To a certain extent this was already happening. Mr Green noted that his daughter was involved in aspects of the family business and did not rule out that this could be where she made a living in the future. However, he commented it was best to 'prepare for all eventualities' and that his daughter might want something different. Pressed on these remarks, Mr and Mrs Green discussed their personal experiences and those of friends and family that had undergone enormous and unexpected change. They identified the need for their daughter to be able to support herself whatever the family circumstances might be and highlighted the economic adaptability that has often been evidenced as a necessity in Gypsy lives (Casa-Nova, 2007; Levinson and Sparkes, 2004; Smith and Greenfields, 2012). Mr Green also hinted that he had ambitions for his daughter to progress her education further but that the transition to secondary school had been very difficult.

The evidence that many Gypsy parents do not want to send their children to school due to experiences of racism, bullying and a lack of cultural understanding (D'Arcy, 2014; Bhopal and Myers, 2008); and, children often drop out early from secondary school or do not make the transition at all (Bhopal and Myers, 2008) was borne out by Mrs Green. She suggested such experiences were typical of many other families living on a nearby local authority site who were not sending their older children to secondary school. Parents on the site were also interviewed for this research and they suggested there had been a gradual building up of dissatisfaction with the school. In particular the head teacher was identified as deliberately wanting to exclude Gypsy students, and, that an equalities liaison officer appointed by the local authority was characterised as being disinterested in Gypsy families. According to Mrs Green,

> They don't want to send their kids to schools if they're going to be bullied or if the teacher is going to pick on them. I can understand that mentality, but at the same time when the parents can't read or write it's the kids that lose out because they then can't read or write and all other people think we are illiterate.

The Greens suggested, and this was confirmed by families on the nearby site, that although children were described as being home educated, in reality they were not receiving any education provision. Most of the families on this site relied on state benefits and were not in employment – meaning there was no, or little, transferral of economic employment skills. Many of these parents did not feel confident or capable to teach their children (often citing illiteracy as a significant barrier to doing so), and were not accessing private tutors due to prohibitive costs. This contrasted dramatically with the Greens, who had adopted all of these strategies and also, in order to circumvent their daughter attending the problematic local state school, had initially enrolled her in another local independent school.

Mr Green, in particular, articulated the importance he identified in obtaining an education. This again seemed linked to understandings of adaptability, but also to a much wider perspective about education as a means of increasing status both within his own Gypsy community but also more widely amongst non-Gypsies.

> When you're not educated, you're seen in a negative light. You're looked down on and people treat you like scum. That's why we have taught Amy from a very early age that she has to get an education, and that if she wants to get on she has to be able to show she can do what the *gaujos*[1] are doing. It's the only way that you will get respected. You hear Gypsies saying they can't read or write. Not old grannies. Grown men, young kids. It's their choice but they don't know any better. They can't read or write and they want an answer why everyone else thinks they're stupid and lazy.

He went on to describe his own daughter's experience.

> Amy went to primary school. She learned the basics. But that's not enough, I wanted her to go on and get GCSEs.[2] Now that's become difficult. But she got the basics and all the Gypsies, they could all get the basics. Primary school, we had some moments, but it was a good school. After that it's much harder.

Whilst Amy regularly attended primary school, she did also experience some form of prejudice from other children despite an initial strategy of being very discrete about the family's Gypsy heritage. According to Mrs Green,

> We didn't make it known that we are Gypsies when Amy went to primary school, but then of course everyone finds out. She's always looks smart, Always in the uniform. Proper shoes. And you can see around here how clean our van is and how clean we are. But there's little kids calling her a 'dirty Gypsy' and that was hard because when they knew we were living in a caravan, they immediately assumed we were dirty and used those stereotypes that *gaujos* have of us.

Despite these negative experiences, Mr and Mrs Green felt it was very important for Amy to continue attending school. They wanted her to get an education and they also wanted to ensure that she had the experience of being able to mix with non-Gypsy children.

> We told Amy that she had to continue to go to school and she was ok with that because she wanted to get an education and wanted to make sure she

56 *Gypsies and Travellers*

was qualified to be able to get a job. Not all the Traveller kids think like that, but we brought her up like that to make sure she was able to read and write and get herself a job – if that's what she wants to do – and she does.

After primary school, Mr and Mrs Green sent Amy to a local, independent school. Mr Green explained that he was already aware of problems with the local state school which had a reputation for racism towards Gypsy students and for a record of routinely excluding Gypsy pupils. He also suggested 'money talks. It talks for me and it talks for the *gaujo*'. He went on to argue,

> My instinct is if I need something I pay top dollar for it. That way I can get the best. So we thought about Amy and we both want her to do well at school. Get her GCSEs. She's bright she could go to university. So she goes to the posh school. They want our cash and we want the best for Amy. If there's a problem it can be sorted out. If she went to (local state school), they're not bothered. I'm not paying them anything.

Unfortunately the Greens felt their expectations were not met by the reality of the school experience. A number of children from families who had attended Amy's primary school also went to her new independent school. The Greens described a fraught few weeks in which Amy was routinely the subject of racist name-calling and also largely excluded from the friendship networks that her peers were developing. Mr Green explained why at this point he decided Amy would be home educated.

> I spoke to the school. They said. Or they suggested we had not let them know that there was a problem with Amy. I said "there's no problem with Amy. Tell me what problem". Nothing to say for themselves. Other parents they complained. You have to guess what they said. The Head Teacher he couldn't tell me what Amy's done. He just thinks (name of school) might not be right for us. Our money was worth less than *gaujo* pounds. You know that? They were never interested in Amy being called names. She never caused any problem at school. And they blamed us, blamed me for not telling them they have kids who hate Gypsies. And racist parents.

Mrs Green continued,

> It's done now. We moved on. But it was a bad time. Amy was upset. Her dad was mad. I couldn't talk about it. We had to fight the school to get the fees back. He (Mr Green) sees schools as being useful but its bollocks isn't it? We both went to primary school and it was hell then, and now it's the same for Amy. The schools aren't for Gypsies. They've never been set up for Gypsies.

Although the Greens' experiences reflected the commonplace encountering of racism in schools as the trigger for their decision to home educate, more

Gypsies and Travellers 57

generally their experience was different to many other Gypsy families. Many Gypsy families who want their children to continue with secondary schooling tend to opt for home education at a slightly later age when they begin to perceive problems associated with adolescence and early-onset adulthood (Myers et al., 2010), often around gendered expectations or concerns about cultural assimilation. This was not the case for the Greens, who in addition to identifying an importance attached to educational achievement also associated this in opposition to traditional Gypsy gender roles. As parents they identified a particular importance for Amy to gain academic credentials and use these to maintain control and power over her life choices. The importance of this outlook was emphasised by the Greens' approach to home education. The family employed several home tutors and continued with her education. At the time of her interviews Amy was intending to take GCSEs in a range of traditional academic subjects (English, Maths, Languages, Sciences and History) including taking English and French a year earlier than the expected requirement. Mr Green explained that although they had received little direct support from the local authority, they had developed a 'strategy' with a former Traveller Education Service (TES)[3] support worker (her current role had been broadened to supporting special educational needs (SEN) students more generally, but she was well known and respected amongst Gypsy families in the area).

> For six months we did nothing. Amy was in the office doing the books or on her phone. Then I spoke to Coleen (TES officer) and we all sat down. I said I don't want Amy in school but also I want her to have the qualifications. Coleen's good. She said you need a strategy. And she introduced us to Mr and Mrs Anders, they tutor all the posh kids round here. And so that was that.

The Anders were retired teachers who offered a range of tutoring services mostly to non-Gypsy parents concerned about their children who were about to take their GCSEs. The strategy involved the Anders agreeing a curriculum for Amy and also providing ongoing hourly tutoring. In addition the Anders had identified other home tutors who were employed by the Greens for particular subjects. The agreed 'strategy' was to ensure Amy did well at GCSEs with the intention that she would then attend a sixth form college to progress on to 'A' Levels.[4] Mr Green reflected on how these events had been unexpected but that they were mostly for the good,

> Amy's very academic. We knew she was bright but you can see it now. I don't mind paying for this and the cost of (independent school) was more than the tutoring. Much more. So why would we live with that? I can't teach her to pass an exam. I can speak French and German and some others but I can't tell her how to get a GCSE in French. That's what schools do. Teachers do. But we can't take the school or the schools can't take Gypsies. It's not their fault they don't understand us. Well it is their fault but I'm not changing the schools. Amy can do well though.

58   *Gypsies and Travellers*

Both the Greens acknowledged that the cost was prohibitive for many families. However, they situated their choices within a narrative of personal responsibilities which were difficult but replicable; and, essentially grounded in their personal business acumen and work ethic. Amy's home tutors, the Anders, spoke very briefly about their perspective and mostly they focused on Amy's potential as a student. Mrs Anders did add however,

> I know three [Gypsy] families who have home educated at different times. None of them wanted to but they all felt for very different reasons it was the only choice left to them. If Amy was in (local state school) now I wonder how well she would be doing. I worked there, seven years ago, and we never had Gypsy children do well. There was always something. Some argument with the school. In retrospect it feels deliberate. They go to school to be failed.

The Greens deployed economic capital in order to improve their child's educational prospects. This was a strategy that they were well placed to pursue and one that they put into practice immediately their daughter was entering secondary schooling. They chose an independent school because of the known concerns other families had expressed about the local state school. This highlights some of the difficulties Gypsy families encounter in regard to the deployment of different capitals (be they economic or social), compared to other families. Their economic capital was seemingly devalued in the context of the independent school; the expectation that by paying for an education the family could insulate itself from the racism of other parents did not materialise. In the Greens' account the school chose to value the capital of other parents more highly. The school could no doubt argue that from a purely business perspective the value of one family's termly fees is worth less than several other families threatening to withdraw their custom. However, the independent school in question markets itself as 'embracing diversity, difference and individuality'; if financial capital was being assessed purely in terms of where does the most money come from, then obviously families from unpopular minority communities would always be liable to exclusion. The Greens' account however of their failure to transfer economic capital as readily as non-Gypsy parents into educational opportunities speaks volumes of the devalued social capital accorded to Gypsies.

The identification of well-known problems associated with local state schools also highlights how social capital materialises differently for Gypsy families. In particular the strong 'bonding' social capital often identified as valuable to a marginalised community (Myers et al., 2010; Putnam, 2000) means that knowledge and expectations of local schools are well known. The accounts of exclusion, racism and name-calling in the local state schools are well understood amongst many families. There is also evidence that the sort of bridging 'social capital' that the Greens identified as being important for Amy's future were not available to the family despite their apparent business success and affluence.

The family encountered an entirely unexpected and negative reaction to Amy's enrolment as a student at the local independent school for example. Later, in order to ensure that Amy did gain access to an education that would provide her with qualifications, the Greens struggled initially because they lacked more effective types of social capital such as a working knowledge of educational systems to ensure Amy made the transitions from being 'home educated' to acquiring qualifications. Mr Green made a very telling point when he distinguished between learning to speak French and successfully taking a French GCSE. Both Mr and Mrs Green are fluent in a number of languages (they were both brought up in bilingual Romany and English families and in their business activities and business travel they have both learned a wide range of European languages), and have passed this knowledge on to their daughter. However, without the intervention and assistance of the TES and the family's home tutors, although Amy would possess the skills to speak and write the language, she would not have the credentials to prove this was the case. The importance that this lack of credentials might have in the future is specifically highlighted by Amy's intention to study languages at university (something her parents support whole-heartedly). The Greens have found a successful strategy to convert their economic capital to overcome deficits in their social and cultural capital which was readily acknowledged by Mr Green. When describing the circumstances which led to Amy being tutored by the Anders, he noted this was largely providential highlighting the difficulty Gypsy families might have in acquiring knowledge of systems and institutions that were not previously accessed by earlier generations of families. It also highlighted the importance of Traveller Education Services as a service that could improve Gypsy families' access to social capital, (though Traveller Education Services are increasing under funded by local authorities). In this vein Mr Green noted that one reason for his engagement in this research was 'to pick your brain'. By which he explained, he wanted to talk about universities with someone who was working in a university; he used the opportunity of 'being researched' to acquire other knowledge that would potentially be useful when Amy applied to university.

The Connor family

The Connor family lived in a fixed trailer on a privately owned site on the outskirts of a Midlands town. The site is situated in close proximity to a motorway on land that is buffered by extensive arable farmland and by a canal. On the opposite bank of the canal is a substantial industrial estate comprising of office blocks and commercial premises. It is a 15-minute drive to the centre of the town and a 5-minute drive to a large supermarket. There are no public transport links to the site. The site itself is largely invisible; the offices on the other side of the canal for example are shielded by landscaped embankments, trees and an industrial fence. There were 10 fixed trailers on the site owned by families who had close family links. The land on which the trailers were situated was separated and shielded from the canal by trees and some low fencing.

60 *Gypsies and Travellers*

The land abutting the canal was used as a work space and social area mostly by younger men and boys.

In part the separation of the land on which the trailers were situated from the canal reflected families' concerns about the safety of smaller children on the site falling in the canal, but it also seemed to reflect the maintenance of privacy between the site residents and the outside world. The interviews were conducted during the summer and there was a steady stream of holidaymakers using the canal for leisure purposes; both river boaters and the site occupants engaged in a fair amount of shared 'hellos' and 'afternoons' and occasional outbursts of good-natured banter. The occasional boat that passed and did not respond was met mostly by the blowing of large raspberries and farting sounds as they departed. Commenting on a particularly jolly family with several waving children, Mr Connor made the succinct point that 'if there wasn't the water between us they'd run a fucking mile'.

The site was accessed via a small, narrow lane that fed off a roundabout that accessed the motorway. There was a large gate at the site entry but this appeared to be always left open for cars and trucks to pass freely onto the site. A considerable amount of rubbish appeared to have accumulated just outside the entrance gate including dismantled car parts and what appeared to be a trailer that had been destroyed. When we visited the site we were greeted by large barking dogs tethered near the first trailer, and this felt as if it was a deliberate means of restricting unwanted access to the site. Many of the trailers on the site appeared to be very old. We spoke to several families living on the site and a picture emerged of families struggling financially. State benefit payments appeared to be the most significant and consistent source of income for most families. Most residents on the site were families with children, and most accessed primary schooling on a fairly regular basis, but very few children of secondary school age attended school.

Mr and Mrs Connor had four children: Billy was 18, Roxanne was 16, Jack was 14 and Sian was 12. Billy was not living on the site. Jack had his own trailer next to the Connors which until recently he had shared with Billy. Roxanne and Sian lived in the family trailer and also another smaller mobile caravan on the family plot.

Mr and Mrs Connor recounted many problems with the local primary schools, including instances of bullying and racism. Their account of their four children's progression through primary school was confusing and consisted of a sequence of arguments and disputes with the school. These resulted in their children being excluded or expelled on a regular basis or being withdrawn by the family. Mrs Connor herself eventually noted that she couldn't remember which dispute related to which child. She discussed how there were often altercations between Gypsy parents and other parents and suggested that the school management were secretly pleased that this happened as they could justify why Gypsies shouldn't be educated. One particular instant however was very clearly discussed by Mrs Connor and seemed to sum up all her feelings about schools.

She described a fight that had taken place between another mother who lived on the site and two other mothers at the local primary school following an accusation of racism being made by the Gypsy mother. At this time

Gypsies and Travellers 61

Jack and Sian were both attending this school and Mrs Connor was picking them up from school. On this particular occasion because an actual physical fight took place on the school grounds, the police were called in. Mrs Connor described how as soon as they knew the police were coming all the Gypsy families including the mother who was involved in the fight, decided to leave. When they arrived the police seemingly arrested three Gypsy mothers, including Mrs Connor, and told them and their children to sit in police cars. This story made the front page of a local newspaper (a copy of which was produced for the researchers to read describing angry parents engaged in scuffles with Gypsies). Mrs Connor described her anger at how the events were reported; in particular she noted that the police never charged any of the Gypsy mothers. Instead all the Gypsies were driven back to the site where the police were offered cups of tea. Close variations of this story were by recounted by all the families living on the site we interviewed. One direct consequence of these events was that all the children attending primary school were withdrawn by the families and arrangements were only slowly made afterwards for children to attend different, less local schools.

For the Connors this experience appeared to define their understanding of schools and relations between schools and Gypsies. Neither Mr Connor nor Mrs Connor had much personal experience of schooling. Mr Connor explained he 'never really went to school' because his parents moved around a lot and also when he did go to school he didn't understand anything. When pressed on this, he discussed being behind in terms of specific skills (e.g. reading and numeracy) but also said about some time spent in a primary school:

> Just being there. I didn't understand what I was supposed to do. It was all sit down, listen, stand up, do this, do it again. It wasn't for me.

Mrs Connor suggested she had never been to school and that was a decision made by her parents. Both Mr and Mrs Connor explained that in many respects going to school was not part of their culture or history. As a consequence of the incident at the primary school, Mrs Connor described herself as being "anti-school".

> The older two didn't go to primary school much. Billy was always going to work with his dad anyway. Roxanne wants to do beauty and she can work with her cousins. So she hasn't missed anything. But we had to send Jack and Sian because the education people came and visited us and said they had been out of school for too long. When they went back, they just got lots of hassle from the other kids calling them names and making them feel like they were nothing. So we took them out, simple as that. When they all went to school in the morning and we all get arrested in the afternoon that was enough.

We discussed how many families who maybe in the past had not chosen schooling were now often choosing to send children to school until they were older.

62 *Gypsies and Travellers*

Mrs Connor agreed that some Gypsy families were doing this and said that she understood why they were doing so. She identified that schools could provide opportunities and knowledge that was unavailable to many Gypsy families through their own networks. Instead, Mrs Connor made it very clear that she was not anti-learning or anti-education, she was anti-school because schools were unable to deal with Gypsy families.

> Even the schools don't know how to deal with us, they treat us like we're a bit of poo floating down the river and they don't think we are important like the other families. I am not against education at all, I think the children should learn things but we teach our children different things for learning. I am anti-school because the school is something that does not understand us and does not want to educate our children.

Jack and Sian had attended school sporadically but had not enjoyed the experience; consequently Mrs Connor was happy to keep them at home when they did not want to attend.

> Because the school was not a good experience for them, I would let them stay at home when they wanted to, but at the same time attend so that we didn't get into trouble. I always knew what I had to do and so did that to keep them [education authority] off my back. For my two eldest nobody ever asked the question – I don't think anybody cared if they went to school. Somethings changed? Everybody wants to know what the Gypsy kids are up to now.

When Jack and Sian reached secondary school age, Mr and Mrs Connor decided they did not want to send them to school. They recounted how other Gypsy and Traveller families were home educating and decided to take this option. They were quite precise on the use of terminology such as 'elective home education'. Mr Connor explained,

> Some of the families here had a talk with the school and the school said, 'you should home educate, if you home educate no one can touch you'. They called it elective home education. E.H.E. And I thought about that and thought that's what we can do. So we decided to not send them to [secondary school] at all and said we were home educating.

When asked what that home education entailed, Mrs Connor said,

> We're not doing it . . . well not as much as we should. We did have a home tutor at the beginning but that was only for about 6 months. I was fighting to get the education authority to pay for the tutor so I had to carry on with the tutor, but they said they wouldn't pay for it, so I just stopped it. I'm not paying for it, I told them.

Gypsies and Travellers 63

This raised the interesting question of what the Connors wanted from a home tutor. Mr Connor explained that the tutor they had employed was supposed to teach their children English, maths and IT skills. He strongly believed this should be provided by the state as his family could not afford tutoring fees. Without a tutor he felt there was a limit to how much he personally could teach his children, but also argued against putting his children 'through school' where they would be unhappy. At the same time he was also very supportive of the choices made by his own parents, in which he engaged with schools on a very marginal basis, arguing that his children could learn enough from within the community just like himself. When asked whether there were some ambiguities in his position, (i.e. both arguing that there were skills that could usefully be gained from education and it was not necessary to access educational opportunities), Mr Connor said, 'basically they don't have to go to school. It's our way. They don't need anything from the school'. In a last effort to unpick the ambiguities in Mr Connor's argument he was asked why he wanted the state to pay for a home tutor if he did not see a great value in the sort of education the tutor would provide, to which he replied, 'if I'm offered something for nothing I'll take it. Everyone here if you offer them a home tutor they'll leap at it but we won't pay for it'.

Mrs Connor suggested that because of the differences in Gypsy lives, schools and local authorities needed to make alternative provision for the education of Gypsy children,

> It is up to the government and the education authority to make sure we are being educated, they look after lots of other families who have some kind of special needs and the government gives them money. So why shouldn't they do the same for us? We're not different to them? But that's the way that we are treated as different from other families who have different needs to ours and that is some kind of prejudice they have against us.

Initially, when Mrs Connor informed the school that she was home educating, she was told the school would inform the local authority. At the time, she was given little support apart from an A4 sheet with links and contacts to home-educating organisations. The main support the Connors identified that would be useful to them was financial assistance but this was not forthcoming. Mrs Connor, backtracking somewhat on her earlier ambivalence about the value of education, argued that,

> You can see we are not from a wealthy background, we struggle and paying for a tutor was another bill for us to pay. I told the Council all of that, but they just kept saying they couldn't help us with that side of it.

The Connors stopped employing a home tutor after six months because they were no longer able to afford his fees. When asked what home education currently looked like for their children, Mrs Connor responded,

> Nothing. We're not educating them.

64 *Gypsies and Travellers*

Mrs Connor went on to say that she was not worried that her children were no longer getting an education. She noted they could both read and write. She also indicated that in many respects her children were getting on with their lives.

> Jack is working with Billy and his dad. He's a toiler so he's making decent money. Sian is happy at home with me and Roxanne. If anyone asks, they are elective home educated. A lot of Gypsy and Traveller families say they are home educating just because they know they can say that, it won't get checked and it means we won't get trouble.

Moving on from our discussion about her own family and home education, Mrs Connor asked about the wider interests of the research. In particular we discussed child safety issues. Mrs Connor identified home education as being very problematic and also very typical of non-Gypsy lives in which people were disconnected from each other. She explained how if she was to physically abuse her children, then her neighbours would intervene if she 'went too far'. She made a specific argument that whilst families left each other alone and didn't interfere in each other's lives, there was an awareness of what was happening in other families and shared expectations about what was acceptable. She compared this to non-Gypsies:

> I can see how that kind of thing would take place because they [education authorities] don't come and visit you, you just have to tell them and that's it. I am sure that is happening in some families but in our communities because there are so many people around all the time, if it was happening someone would know. When you know people properly you can stop them.

Despite her own experiences, Mrs Connor felt that more regulation should be put in place for parents who chose to home educate.

> I think there should be two things that they [education authorities] should be thinking about. They should ensure that they give the families some kind of help. That could be paying for tutors to do their job. And they should also make sure that they check and visit the families to make sure that everything is alright, then you wouldn't get those cases of children being treated badly.

Conclusions

These two case studies demonstrate different attitudes of Gypsy families who are home educating. There is evidence highlighting both the rapid increase in numbers of Gypsies attending school (Myers and Bhopal, 2009) and also the increasing importance attached to education (D'Arcy, 2014). This reflects the economic demands of changing economies and also in some respects the

Gypsies and Travellers 65

positive approaches of some schools and local authorities to provide accessible education. However home education remains a common choice for many Gypsy families.

Gypsy families who choose to home educate do so for various reasons. However, those decisions almost invariably are shaped in some degree by racism experienced when accessing schools; either from children and parents or from teaching staff. Whilst they might share similar experiences to other non-Gypsy families, the practical experience of becoming a home educator was invariably shaped by managing educational choices as a Gypsy. This is highlighted by the example of the Greens who initially looked towards an independent school as the best opportunity for their daughter. This was a choice shaped by concerns about the local state school's very poor reputation for educating Gypsies. It was not a choice that most families can make; the high cost of private schooling in the UK is prohibitive. By making this choice, the Greens were also identifying the wider benefits of independent schools as a means of achieving better academically. The failure of the Greens' strategy of engaging with education through the free-market economy rather than state provision is indicative that Gypsies encounter a systemic, structural fault-line in their relationship to education. This begins to explain why home education has always been a relatively common or traditional route adopted by many Gypsy families. It's not simply the case that Gypsy families are somehow unwilling to engage with schools based on their cultural predispositions. Rather what is evidenced is a range of difficulties and barriers designed to dissuade Gypsy children from accessing schools. The Greens' experience was markedly different from that of other wealthy non-Gypsy families who deploy their financial capital to buy their children a better education. In principle independent schools operating within a free-market economy should value a Gypsy pound as highly as a non-Gypsy pound, but the Greens felt this was not the case.

Traumatic moments are a touchstone of Gypsy accounts of choosing home education. The Greens' rejection by the independent school bears a close resemblance to the emotional impact of the day Mrs Connor and other Gypsy mothers were taken away from their children's school by police. Both of these were extreme instances but almost every family we interviewed offered accounts of a moment that was 'the last straw' or 'after that we couldn't take it any more' or 'I couldn't send him back into that'. Generally these accounts related to instances of racism, name-calling and bullying, but they were also set against a backdrop in which Gypsy culture was not represented in the school or in which families felt something of their children's culture was being lost or appropriated in the process of attending school. It was interesting to note the regularity with which the wider account of difficulties or discontent with school environments were effectively tolerated until the family hit a single traumatic moment.

In some respects the Connor parents appeared to present a fairly *blasé* attitude towards schooling, often making the case that there was little for their children to gain from education. Home education was presented as being a way of side-stepping authority. And yet the family had still made efforts to engage with schools; and, for all the anger at the police arriving at the school, the family had later enrolled their youngest daughter in another primary school that was further away from their home. Later they went on to invest some of their own limited resources in a home tutor and were passionate in arguing for funding for a tutor. One conclusion was that the Connors identified the value that could be derived from schools, but faced with insurmountable difficulties in attending school, they adopted a highly personalised moral high ground: their misgivings at the loss of educational opportunities overwritten with pride at the effectiveness of traditional Gypsy cultural practice.

The Greens and the Connors had very distinct attitudes towards their children's education; the Greens clearly seeing a value in the academic opportunities whilst the Connors identified more utilitarian advantages. However, by far the biggest difference between the families was their wealth differential. Unlike the Connor family, the Greens were financially positioned to access all the advantages of successful middle-class families generally. Despite their differences in outlook and financial resources, both families seemed destined to only access home education.

Notes

1 *Gaujo* is a term used by Gypsies and Travellers to describe non-Gypsies.
2 GCSEs (General Certificate of Secondary Education) are public exams taken by 16 year olds in England.
3 The TES (Traveller Education Service) supports the educational needs of nomadic families in England and receives funding from local government.
4 'A' levels (advanced level) are exams taken in England at age 18 which are required for entrance into UK higher education.

6 Religion

'We want our children to learn specific values'

There are numerous accounts of home education being particularly attractive to families with strong religious beliefs (Arai, 2000; Cooper and Sureau, 2007; Stevens, 2009). Homeschooling in the United States is dominated by evangelical Christians, generally with traditional, right-wing family values, who characterise education in terms of being a parental rather than a state responsibility (Arai, 2000). The picture that emerged from interviewing religious families in the United Kingdom was slightly different. Prioritising family needs and community bonding were often stressed as factors influencing the choice of home education. However, the terms in which such choices were made were often less doctrinal. Both Muslim and Christian families identified value in schooling, but tended to cite shortcomings around the provision of education, issues of safety and concerns about ethical content, rather than suggesting that it was solely a parental responsibility to manage the education of their children. The type of home education provided for children was also often very different. In particular home education in many respects became understood as an administrative category for some Muslim families who were choosing to access locally sympathetic non-state schools. Slightly different priorities emerged for some Plymouth Brethren families who used home education as a means of bypassing what they felt were inappropriate primary schools with a view to their children entering secondary faith schools at a later date. One interviewee, a former Jehovah Witness, described how her parents identified little value in education and schooling generally, in many respects regarding it as a distraction from the more important religious life to be lived in heaven. She clearly identified the failings of such an education which did not address the 'earthly' essentials that comprise both the acquisition of basic academic skills and the wider socialisation associated with mixing with different children.

This chapter explores the experiences of an evangelical Christian family and a Muslim family who adopted home education as a means of delivering an education that promotes their cultural values and also promotes what Putnam (2000) describes as bonding social capital. In many ways this process reflects a risk management strategy that appeals directly to minority communities, particularly minority communities who feel their culture or world is 'at risk'. This has been evidenced in Gypsy families' wider engagement with schools

68   *Religion*

(Myers et al., 2010), as well as in their decisions to home educate (Bhopal and Myers, 2016). This highlights a very different experience to that of traditional American evangelical families for whom homeschooling is potentially a more outward-looking engagement with the world (Apple, 2006a, 2015; Stevens, 2002). An engagement that both politically and socially reflects prevailing moods within American society in which right-wing, evangelical lifestyles are identifiable as conventional. This chapter considers two families for whom a deep engagement with their religious values and the communities in which those values are embedded, shaped their decisions to home educate.

The Smith family

The Plymouth Brethren are a conservative Evangelical Christian movement for whom the Bible is considered to be the word of God and the foundation for the authority of the church. The Plymouth Brethren consists of a network of organisations who form assemblies or small churches to worship together as a collective. All individuals who are part of the collective see themselves as 'Brethren'. Two fundamentally distinct branches of the Plymouth Brethren congregate in the UK; these are generally described as being either 'open' or 'exclusive' gatherings. Open Brethren gatherings (or assemblies) are based on individuals who share the same beliefs as independent local churches. Exclusive Brethren are not obliged to recognise and adhere to the disciplinary actions of the other associated assemblies. Disciplinary action includes attending church every Sunday and breaking bread as a ritual, as well as singing, teaching and taking communion. Dissenting family members, (i.e. those who do not abide by the strict codes and practices of the Brethren which might include not living according to Scriptures, being gay, engaging in adultery or pre-marital sex), have been known to be isolated within the family or ostracised entirely (e.g. not being allowed to speak to them or even shake their hand).

Open Brethren churches sometimes collaborate with other Christian churches, holding joint Gospel and religious events or other activities in partnership with non-Brethren churches who share their Evangelical Christian beliefs. However, those who tend to be more conservative in their views are less likely to want to mix with others outside of their own church.

The Smith family are members of an open Brethren congregation who live in the Home Counties in a small suburban village on the outskirts of a small town. The 'village' is one of several localities identified by residents as being distinct and separate from the wider 'town' identity. However as an outsider it can be difficult to distinguish these local boundaries; town and village appear to have merged into each other within a single suburban sprawl. The area is predominantly White with a mixture of families from middle- and working-class backgrounds. There are several schools in the area including both primary and secondary Church of England faith schools. The village is identified as being geographically the home for a number of Plymouth Brethren families who live in relative proximity to each other along a series of streets with noticeably greater numbers of larger, detached houses.

The Smiths lived in one such house and described themselves as being members of the local Brethren church. In the opening moments of his interview Mr Smith acknowledged and discussed the differences between Exclusive and Open Brethren in response to a question about the Brethren generally. However, whilst he acknowledged that the interviewer may have some conversant knowledge about the Brethren, he went on to describe a more nuanced and personal depiction of his religious identity,

> We tend to see ourselves as being able to practice what we believe, we are open because we will attend events with other Christians. And we work with two charities in [the town] with other Christians. But, we are also exclusive. In a personal sense. In our private, family life. Our children are very important members of our community. They are the future and as a community we look after our children in everyone's best interests. They don't always need to mix ... there may be times when it is beneficial not to learn with others who don't follow our scriptures or our doctrine.

The Smiths had sent their children to a non-faith school graded as 'good' by OFSTED. The school has a large number of children described as having special educational needs and the school is well known for its inclusive education policies. Whilst the surrounding area of the school is predominantly White, the school itself is relatively mixed with children from different ethnic backgrounds and different social classes. Historically this school has provided school places to Plymouth Brethren families in the area and teachers are acknowledged to have built a good *rapport* with Brethren families over many years.

Discussing the distinctiveness and difference of Plymouth Brethren in the locality, Mr Smith noted that,

> It is true that people see us differently. There is often a picture painted of Brethren living their lives in isolation from the world. This is untrue. We have pastoral responsibilities for all our Brethren, our families and for the communities we live amongst.

Mr Smith described how he and other Brethren families worked closely with two local charities (not associated directly with the Plymouth Brethren). He described a recent period when for several weeks it had become very cold and that this appeared to have coincided with an increase in the numbers of homeless people living on the street that were in need of emergency help. He described this sort of work as being related both to his Christian beliefs and also as evidence of an engagement with the wider community. Discussing the Brethren's reputation for insularity, he suggested the Brethren shared 'core beliefs' that were only understood within the Brethren whilst still understanding the wider community.

70   *Religion*

The Smiths along with five other Plymouth Brethren families had sent their children to a local primary school throughout the past seven years. Often the children would be dropped off together and the families were easily recognisable. Generally the mothers, dressed in long skirts with scarfs on their heads, took their children to school. One of the reasons that the Smiths were initially happy with the school was because there were other children from their church attending. The Smiths had three children, Mark was 9, Jessica was 8 and Matthew was 6. Mrs Smith explained,

> We sent our children to the school because we knew the other families. From our church. It's a very good school with very committed teachers. When our children were at the school they understood our concerns. They understood we want our children to do well. Also some of the things we allow our children to do.

Mr Smith discussed how the school was aware of Brethren customs and did their best to ensure the families were included and seen as part of the school. For example, the school had been accommodating when ensuring Brethren children were able to eat separately or go home for lunch in accordance with parental wishes. Children were also not allowed to engage in sex education and there were certain activities that parents did not want their children to participate in. One such activity was an annual dance festival in which children from different local schools with an interest in dance could participate. This culminated in a public performance widely attended by parents. Mrs Smith suggested that she personally felt uncomfortable with some of the dance routines and costumes; she also highlighted how the school had been effective in communicating information about the event. In many respects the Smiths described a pattern in which their children attended the local primary school, whilst also maintaining some distance from other families.

> We do send our children to the school but at the same time we want them to remain true to the Lordship of Christ. That means we can place burdens on our children. On all of us. These are important choices about our lives.

Asked to explain what this meant in practice, Mr Smith suggested that some activities that other families considered to be 'ordinary' might be difficult for them, particularly their children, to engage in. Spending time in other children's houses after school or attending birthday parties for example would not be allowed. These restrictions included other (non-Brethren) Christian families, because,

> We share different beliefs. God employs me to promote eternal salvation. God also employs me to protect and foster my family. We are all very close.

The Smiths decided to home educate in large part because the numbers of other Brethren children attending the school fell dramatically over a two-year period. This happened because several other families' children transitioned to secondary school coinciding with another Brethren family deciding to home educate. The Smiths, like many other Brethren families in the area, planned for their own children to attend a Plymouth Brethren faith-based secondary school. Home education for the remainder of their primary schooling was therefore seen as a temporary measure. Mrs Smith explained that although she still had very positive feelings about the school, she had concerns about her children becoming isolated.

> When the other children started to leave. I was worried. I worried my children might not have anyone else that they could play with or be friends with and they would be alone. So then we decided we would take them out of school and I would educate them myself at home.

Mrs Smith informed the school of her intentions of educating at home. She did receive some support in terms of access to curriculum materials and advice about local home education support groups, but in large part the family did not feel the support offered was necessarily of any value,

> The school did give me information on the curriculum and how to contact organisations that could give me support. But we didn't necessarily need any of that. Our congregation always supports families. That was always important. And as a family we place a lot of our hope in our children's futures. In everything that makes up their education. And that has not changed. I would never say it was a relief to be able to take the children out and keep them at home. But it did mean we could organise within our family. Prioritise the things that are important.

Taking her children out of school gave Mrs Smith the opportunity to structure her children's learning and this enabled her to focus all her teaching from a religious perspective.

> I take the scriptures and use them to inform what I am teaching the children, so then I can ensure they are learning our way of life through the Bible but they are also being taught what they need to know. That is never easy but it is how we always live our life. I feel the knowledge our children need is knowledge that grows out of God's love and wisdom. That is freely available. So perhaps our children's education remains the same however we choose to move forward. The school was very caring. The teachers worked hard to foster all the children. We never felt they let our children down or that they worked against our belief in God. There are still moments when my husband or myself would have to explain how there might be better ways to live. Choosing to home educate makes that simpler. Our church is our first port of call.

Mrs Smith outlined a range of different support mechanisms that operated as a result of her association with the Plymouth Brethren. At a local level this

72 *Religion*

included the support and guidance of her local congregation. In addition she was actively involved in an informal support network of other home educating Brethren families who attended the same congregation. She also described how there was some provision of educational materials available from the wider church organisation. However, she often returned to discussions of the responsibilities her family and congregation felt for their children's upbringing. She described how this merged on some occasions with her families' business interests. The Smiths owned a successful building and land development business which employed around 30 permanent staff. The company maintained a long-standing commitment to several charities in Africa which involved using their skills in project development to build schools and housing in several remote villages. Mrs Smith explained how one aspect of her children's home education had been to spend six weeks in Africa with her husband and herself when the firm sent over a contingent of their staff to complete the building of new school buildings.

> I'm sure we could have agreed those arrangements with the school but in a lot of respects it made that decision easier. For our children, to see how we can do God's work in a very real way was important for all of us. It makes a difference to their understanding of their lives in this world. The school could never provide that education.

For the Smiths such experiences combined with the close networks at home meant they did not have any concerns about the socialisation aspects of their children's upbringing.

> I don't see that aspect as a negative issue, I see it as the opposite. It is very important for our children to mix with other children and families. It is also important they mix with children and adults who have the same values. They learn so much through our church and through our own family. That's important and because we are so close and so committed as a family and as a church they learn about the world. They see how living by the scriptures and how living within the word of God is not a limiting thing at all. It's the opposite.

The Smiths intended sending all their children to a Plymouth Brethren secondary school when they reached year 7. This reflected the plans of other congregation members and various well-established communal arrangements were in place to assist with transport to the school which fell a little way out of their local catchment area. Mr Smith noted that,

> We wouldn't be able to teach them everything they need when they reach secondary school. We still are responsible for their education and we are still engaged in their education. We still bring our love and guidance and we are still their parents so their education is part of our whole life. But it

Religion 73

is harder. They need to make sure they are taught the curriculum for their GCSE exams and we are not qualified to do that. There are many Plymouth Brethren schools that provide a solid religious foundation and many have good GCSE results.

Mrs Smith also described how the transition to secondary school was in effect an extension of their commitment to both their children's learning and also to their wider religious upbringing,

> The [Brethren] school is very good and we know it so well from other families. The church has always invested in these schools. The teachers are very capable and they bring out the best in our children. I don't feel I should be afraid for my children. They have Christ and the church so they are very strong people. The school means they will learn other skills and will do so much in the future.

The Smiths were clearly very committed to their religious beliefs. The choice to home educate whilst the children remained at primary school reflected a range of concerns about the school environment which was changing due to generational change amongst other Brethren families. It also seemed driven by choices being made by other families to home educate. Both Mr and Mrs Smith gave an impression of being highly independently minded about their life choices and about their responsibilities as parents. When asked directly whether or not their church placed pressure on them to home educate, Mr Smith described a more complex relationship, replying:

> No. It's more important that we find our own path. We love God and we love our children. We will do the best for them. We share our hopes for all the children. They are the future and our church supports that. At different times that might mean we make different choices. Our congregation has always supported [primary] school in its work.

The Smiths' experience was in many respects made easier by their heavy investment in both a spiritually understood lifestyle and also within the institutions of their church. Spiritually they felt they were making good effective choices; and whilst these might diverge from the decisions made by many other families, they expressed a degree of confidence in their choices which might have been harder to make for other families who did not have access to the same supportive levels of community. The support networks of the wider church and other families in their congregation provided both the practical day-to-day advice and knowledge needed to successfully manage a home-educating regime and also a more over-arching setting in which they could imagine how the lives of their children would develop in the future. Their own business interests, which were closely allied ethically to their religious affiliations, also provided a solid financial basis on which to be home educators. The intersections between

74 *Religion*

business activities, religion and charity work suggested they could access a broad spread of social and community engagement.

In many respect the Smiths were in an enviable position of being able to manage the home education of their children very effectively. They drew upon well-established economic, cultural and social capital to implement a successful range of strategies. Despite this, a question mark seemed to remain over the actual trigger to make the decision not to leave their children in primary school. Bearing in mind the Smiths' own description of the school being supportive and having a longstanding relationship with Brethren families and the family's commitment to their children's education, the decision to cease schooling raised some questions. The Smiths indicated that the sudden decrease in numbers of other Brethren children attending and the decision of other families to home educate were probably the prime motivations for home educating.

In many respects the school and local authorities' response to the decision was perhaps surprisingly low-key. The Smiths explained how it was a decision that was acknowledged and some small efforts made to offer support, but there was little concern raised that a largish family should choose to make this choice. This possibly reflected the primary schools own longstanding understandings of Brethren families as largely engaged and actively responsible for their children's education.

The Khan family

The Khan family had four children aged 12, 10, 9 and 7. Mr and Mrs Khan were devout Muslims and described their religion as a way of life for their whole family. In many respects their adoption of some aspects of home education mirrored that of the Smith family. Although as a family they had more limited access to economic, social and cultural capital, they still made similar decisions about deploying these resources in a way that protected their children's education within a wider umbrella of community concern. The main element missing from their current strategies was the transition to providing an effective secondary education despite acknowledging the need for a broader curriculum-based education. Their eldest daughter who could have attended secondary school was still being home educated along with her younger (primary school aged) siblings. All the children had attended a local primary school in the past but at the time of the interviews were being home educated.

Both parents had been born in the UK and brought up as Muslims by their parents who came to the UK from Pakistan over 30 years ago. The parents had a marriage that was arranged by their families and this reflected their position as a 'traditional' Asian family. Both Mr and Mrs Khan initially sent their children to their local primary school which was located in an inner city London borough. The borough in which they lived is one of the poorest boroughs in the country, in which unemployment is high and children who attend the local secondary catchment school are less likely than the national average to obtain 5 GCSEs.

Religion 75

Both Mr and Mrs Khan and their extended families lived in and around the same locality all their lives. The Khans lived in an area that is predominantly Asian and this was reflected in a school population that included high numbers of minority ethnic children (including many from Muslim backgrounds).

Mrs Khan had trained as a human resources assistant and her husband worked as an accountant for an insurance company. Mrs Khan worked locally and Mr Khan worked in central London. The Khans' extended family all lived close by and Mrs Khan's mother and sister in particular shared the family's childcare arrangements.

Mr and Mrs Khan identified their historic concerns about their local primary school in terms of its performance and engagement with parents. They identified that whilst it was not a 'failing' school or a particularly poor school compared to other local choices, it was also not a hugely successful or ambitious school (Mr. Khan suggested that the lack of ambition of schools locally was a general problem). Mrs. Khan also suggested the school was generally disengaged from parents and that, 'they don't know me, we are anonymous'. Both parents raised concerns that the school was going to increase from a three- to four-class intake and that this increase in size would only exacerbate existing problems. Some of these concerns were mirrored in the schools most recent OFSTED report which, although it ranked the school as 'good', highlighted problems around staff turnover, teaching quality and pupil achievement.

Despite their dissatisfaction, Mr and Mrs Khan had continued sending their children to the school, in large part for practical reasons associated with childcare and ensuring their children were receiving an education. This changed following the November 2015 terrorist attacks in Paris. After these incidents there had been a succession of playground incidents and name-calling in which Muslim children (including the Khans) were described as terrorists. The Khans' felt the school response was ineffective and often characterised by mild reprimands of offenders and a *softly, softly* approach in which victims and name-callers were called upon to discuss and reflect what constituted good behaviour. Mr Khan suggested,

> The teachers prefer to think everyone is a big happy family and everything is good if no one says anything is bad . . . they prefer an easy life. But, my children are unhappy. My children need someone, need the teacher to say 'No. We don't behave this way'. But they don't do that.

In addition there had also been several instances of parents being verbally abusive to some of the Muslim parents. Whilst this had not directly affected the Khans or their extended family, they felt very upset and threatened by these events. In particular they highlighted that the school again dealt with what the Khans considered to be very serious problems, in a too light-handed or conciliatory fashion. Set against the general dissatisfaction with the school, these events were the trigger for deciding to home educate all four of their children

76 *Religion*

(all of whom at that stage were attending primary school). Mrs Khan described how their initial response had been to identify another, more suitable school.

> I was worried when I heard the parents and the kids saying things like all the Muslims are terrorists, they just upset me. I was thinking I might change schools for the kids anyway, they were not really learning that much so then we just thought let's take them out and send them to another school. My sister was talking to someone at the school and they said they also knew some other Asian families who were home educating and we found out and found this group who do it all together.

Mrs Khan found a group of Muslim women who were all from semi-professional backgrounds who had decided to home educate their children. Most of the mothers were dissatisfied with the education their children were receiving, mainly due to the lack of religious content they were receiving.

> I know it's not the responsibility of the school to teach about religion, especially about Muslim religion because there are lots of stereotypes about what it means to be a Muslim. Lots of people just assume that you are a terrorist and don't understand that we are not like that. Our religion does not tell us to kill innocent people and to think that's what people think about us is very upsetting.

Mrs Khan spoke about how she wanted her children to have knowledge about Islam and the Quran. Her children already received Islamic teaching as they spent time each weekend in a *madrassa* in their local mosque. But, to have religious teaching as part of their everyday education was seen as positive and attractive to her.

> When I knew there was a group of women who were home educating and they were doing it in a way that included the religious teachings of Islam, I was very excited and I found out about it. They are all very serious and they take the religious side of it and the education side of it very seriously. So it means the children can have the best of both worlds and feel proud about their heritage.

Mrs Khan felt that she was able to share the education of her children with others who had similar values to her own. Her religious values were shared and seen as part of the educational experience for her children. The support she received from this group of home educators was vital; without it, she would not choose to home educate.

> To be honest, now if I didn't have the support of the group, I don't think I could do it on a long term basis. You need the support, someone to share

stuff with and also the kids need to mix with other kids. This way, it means they have the best of both worlds. They mix with kids who are like them and I think they get that individual attention that they would never get in the class from the teacher.

Whilst Mrs Khan did think it was the state's responsibility to provide her children with an education, she thought that once parents had taken their children out of school then the responsibility was up to the parent.

I think if you decide to take your child out of school, you are saying that you don't trust the school to provide an education for your child and you have to do it yourself. Part of me thinks the school should support you in this, but part of me thinks the school will say we can educate the child at school so you don't need to do this at home.

Asked whether she thought she should receive some financial support for home educating her children, Mrs Khan was unsure of her position. In some ways this indicated a surprising lack of awareness of the legality and procedures around home education. Most other home educators we spoke to had a very clear picture of their standing (generally described as a lack of standing), in relation to educational support. The Khans were also unusual in not having come across the official jargon term 'elective home education'. Mrs Khan explained,

I am not sure, what kind of financial support can you ask for? For books, pens or other materials? I don't think you can ask for payment for a tutor because I think if you decide to take your child out of school you have to be able to provide them with that education. I don't think you have to be a teacher but you have to be able to teach them, otherwise you should leave them to be educated by the teachers in the schools.

In addition to some uncertainties about home education itself, Mrs Khan was unsure as to how long she was going to home educate her children. She clearly identified limitations in her current strategy as her children got older,

I think I am comfortable keeping them at home and educating them here whilst they are primary school age, but I don't feel so confident for secondary schooling. I think that is more serious and you have to have a qualified teacher to teach them the proper subjects and it leads to their GCSEs so you have to make sure they get the right education for that.

When asked about her eldest 12-year-old daughter's education, Mrs Khan suggested the family was weighing up their options. They had identified the possibility of attending an Independent Islamic school but no secondary state faith schools were accessible to the family. When pressed on whether or not

78   *Religion*

her eldest daughter was receiving the sort of education she might identify as being suitable at secondary school level, Mrs Khan suggested they would "wait and see" how she progressed with her current home education arrangements. Mrs Khan confirmed that the local authority had not put any pressure on the family to return to schooling, including in relation to her elder daughter possibly making the transition back to secondary school.

In our wider discussions we described to the Khans how other Muslim families we had interviewed for this research used privately run *madrassas* as an additional support for their home education, perhaps accessing them on a part-time basis or using them as a full-time alternative to schooling. Mr and Mrs Khan both outlined their concerns about the cost of such arrangements and also described how some of smaller, privately run institutions were particularly badly organised, did not offer a well-rounded education and were not felt to be a good alternative. The Khans had identified one Independent Islamic school which offered a good quality of education and did not charge the high level of fees associated with private schooling generally; but they were unhappy with the travel arrangements that would need to be made in order that their daughter could attend that particular school. Concerns about travel arrangements were raised both in relation to their oldest child travelling alone to secondary school (a journey time of 45–60 minutes that would have relied on public transport), and also in discussions about alternative primary schools that were considerably closer but still entailed using buses. Mrs Khan suggested it might be more 'practical' in the future if more than one child travelled together to secondary school; when pressed on what she meant by practical, Mrs Khan said she would feel 'more comfortable' about safety fears for her children.

Looking ahead to the options their children might have for a secondary education, the Khans wanted this teaching to take place in an environment where they felt comfortable and where they were sure that their children would learn the correct moral and religious codes of being a Muslim. They wanted their children to be proud of being a Muslim and emphasised the importance of this in the current climate.

> The kids have to be proud of being Muslim. These days people are scared and afraid of admitting that they are Muslim because there are so many negative stereotypes attached to that label. The media and everyone else seems to think that *all* Muslims are the problem [original emphasis] but that is clearly not the case.

Mrs Khan on the one hand knew the advantages of sending her children to a Muslim faith school but she was also aware of the disadvantages.

> We want them to go to a Muslim faith school when they reach secondary school age. The children know what they have to do and they get on with it. They are mixing with other kids who are like them and who have the

same values. I would like them to mix with other kids from white, black and other Asian backgrounds but I think that might be dangerous for them.

Mrs Khan worried that her daughters may become influenced by Western moral codes and want to have boyfriends, drink alcohol or rebel. She felt that a Muslim faith school might in many respects solve a lot of the concerns her decision to home educate was intended to tackle. In many respects either option was simply a restatement or enactment of the family's religious faith and engagement in their local community, for example in defining gender roles.

> We pray separately anyway and the schools teach the children very high moral codes and keep the boys and girls separate anyway. The advantage of the schools is that it reminds the girls about their ancestry and who they are. They have to know there are certain expectations placed upon them if they are Muslim, but this isn't something that we say to them, it's something that they know from an early age.

Mrs Khan identified some concerns she felt about her children attending Muslim schools because of the lack of diversity. However, she also described the advantages, mostly those centred around child safety, that were derived from this approach.

> When we teach the kids at home, they are only taught with other Muslim kids and when they go to Muslim faith schools they are only taught with other Muslims. I know this is not perfect as it could give the children a distorted picture of what really happens in society but it protects them from the prejudice and racism they will get because they are Muslim.

For Mrs Khan the advantages of home education and Muslim faith schools far outweighed the disadvantages of attending non-faith state schools. If anything, she suggested she would have liked to have educated her children at home from an early age.

> Because of the different support we have with the other families, I could have educated the children at home and not sent them to school at all. I think this would have been good because they would have just received a Muslim type of education. But on the other hand, they might find it harder to mix with other children and not understand that people are different.

The overriding concern expressed by the Khans was the need to ensure the safety of their children at a time of increasing hostility directed towards Muslims. Mr and Mrs Khan made the decision to home educate their children on the basis of a number of competing priorities. They wanted their children to have a positive experience of education and also to protect them from what

80 *Religion*

they regarded as immoral aspects of Western culture and also what they perceived as racist stereotyping.

> I do see it as a sort of protection for my children. I am shielding them from all the negative things that go on in society and in schools. I am shielding them from having to experience racism and having to be told they are terrorists and that is my main reason for doing it.

Whilst they wanted their children to mix with different children, their religious and community allegiances appeared to take priority. Home education was a means of focusing their children's education within a narrow community field shaped by shared religious practice, shared used of Urdu as a language of choice and extended family and community links. Despite the acknowledgement of very effective secondary faith schools, the family still prioritised educational strategies embedded in these shared, and very local, home education practices. There did not appear to be any urgency in sending their elder daughter to secondary school. In many respects, and in particular bearing in mind the family's own identification of their inability to provide the educational support necessary at GCSE level, this clashed with Mrs Khan's hopes that in the future, all her children would go to university. Mrs Khan described the need for her girls to cope with stereotypes in British society about Muslim girls gendered lives:

> There are stereotypes of the things people think about Muslim women and most of them are incorrect. We are taught to be strong. We are taught that education is a good thing for everyone, especially for women. We are not taught to be submissive. It is important to know that Islamic teachings and the Quran do not say that. It is the stereotypes that people have of us.

Conclusions

Despite having different experiences of the effectiveness of primary schooling, both the Khan and Smith family adopted remarkably similar strategies when deciding to home educate their children. They both became involved with networks of other local home educators who shared their religious beliefs and a common understanding of collective community. One reading for these actions is that they represent a retreat from an engagement with wider, more diverse groups of people. In this respect we might identify a moment in which communities choose to rely on more inward-looking bonding social capital rather than developing outward-facing bridging social capital (Putnam et al., 2004). One noticeable difference between the two families was the seeming fatalism of the Khans in their apparent failure to plan for the future. Whilst the Smiths had a clearly identifiable (and practical) understanding of what their children would do come secondary school age, the Khans appeared almost to be coasting with no real strategy in place. This was despite the family's identification of the impossibilities of equipping their eldest daughter with all the educational skills they felt she would need in the future. In part this seemed to be a gendered decision. Possibly if their oldest child was a boy, then a more robust attitude would be taken to their travelling on public transport to an independent faith school. In part it may also have been an issue created around class and a lack of economic, social and cultural capital; there was a suspicion, unconfirmed by the Khans, that they would possibly struggle with the financial implications of four children attending an independent school. At the same time there was perhaps a failure to identify more suitable state schooling options.

Anthony Giddens notes that although 'risk' is an understanding of the future, it is 'related to present practices' (1991: 117). The Smiths seemed engaged in an inward-looking moment prior to their children going to secondary school. A range of risks was associated with their children, including how they could engage beyond the narrowest confines of their community whilst still maintaining a strong religious identity. The withdrawal of their children from school can easily be read as demonstrating the family's insularity; but it was also a clearly transitory measure, and one that was tempered by religious activities that went beyond the most private aspects of family life. The Khans' decision however seemed in some respects to have left their children somewhat stranded with few options to move on. This was not the case for all the Muslim families we interviewed. Another Muslim family who could be characterised as being more middle-class and who had access to a wider range of social and capital (the mother was a teacher and the father a university lecturer), when faced with similar issues of name-calling and bullying at school, put in place a similar strategy to that of the Smiths. They home educated their primary school-aged children in the short term but identified state secondary schools that appeared to cater for a more diverse ranges of pupils and would better suit their children in the future. This same family also had significantly greater access to economic capital and was actively considering and able to move house in order to ensure they were resident in the (more expensive) catchment area for these schools. Other Muslim families we interviewed adopted the mantle of 'elective home education' but managed their children's education through *madrassa* schools; all of these families were characterised by being poorer and having restricted access to social or cultural capital within their family and community networks.

One difference for the Khans and other Muslim families was that their decision to home educate was framed within a discourse in which their religious beliefs were associated with being a potential risk. This occurred quite specifically in 2015 following OFSTED's investigations into the Trojan Horse affair in Birmingham when some Muslim faith schools were accused of teaching a narrow Islam-centric curriculum that potentially undermined British values (Myers and Bhopal, 2018). Muslim families were explicitly identified by OFSTED as using the loose regulation around home education as 'cover' for accessing such illegal, unregistered *madrassa* schools (OFSTED, 2015b, 2016). Douglas and Wildavsky describe how the 'perception of risk is a social process' (1982: 6) in which different societies often choose which risks to highlight and which to ignore reflecting their social customs. In the context of global risks

82   *Religion*

that traverse national borders that Beck (1992) describes, the threat of radicalisation or Islamification materialises in stark terms as the division between Western secular or Christian outlooks and the new risk of a Muslim 'other' posing as a home educator. This is problematic for Muslim families who, like their non-Muslim neighbours, are also reflexive agents (Beck, 1992, 2006), faced with managing the same local risks for their children's education, including those of failing schools or racist bullying; and, simultaneously needing to situate their strategies within global discourses that they, personally, are potential threats to British 'values' and British society. For the Plymouth Brethren families, there was no comparable identification that their religious outlook posed an implicit threat to society; they may well have been viewed in terms of their difference but the only risks that were identified around their choices were generic risks associated with their children's personal education. The same was true to an even greater extent for other religious home educators associated with more traditional or mainstream UK churches. This also highlights differences between perceptions of homeschooling in the United States which are often associated with a shift towards right-wing ideological standpoints; and the UK, where generally home education is viewed as a politically non-partisan practice.

Whilst it is impossible to predict the future, social class, access to economic and social capital, all seemed likely to ensure families could plan better educational outcomes for their children. They also seemed related to opportunities in the future for families, and children in particular, to develop the types of bridging social capital identified by Putnam et al. (2004). So whilst for a short period the Smiths' children were undoubtedly experiencing a more restrictive, community led, inward-looking educational experience, they would at a later date transfer to the Plymouth Brethren faith school which employed teachers with a range of religious views; they were more likely to acquire the academic skills that would result in their going to university; and, in the short term their family engagement in business and charitable activities ensured some degree of engagement beyond just the close-knit community of their congregation. There was a clear suspicion that the Khan children were simply not engaging beyond a very narrow band of close community members.

7 Special educational needs and disability

'Most schools don't want and have never wanted our children'

This chapter highlights the concerns of families whose children have special educational needs or disabilities within the context of schooling. It concentrates on the experiences of two families whose children had identifiable medical conditions, both of whom felt the specific needs of their children were not adequately supported by state schooling. Such narratives tend to situate themselves within sympathetic accounts of families' managing risk, often made all the more sympathetic because of failings of local authorities to deliver an 'inclusive' education.

Other families also cited special needs related to their children either in terms of their very specific abilities or in a more generalisable sense of 'every child is special'. One of the more general conclusions of our research was that home educators often develop the argument of 'specialness' in relation to their child in order to justify or explain their decisions for their child. Assessing the validity or scale of the individual 'specialness' of children was largely beyond the scope of our research and in many circumstances seemed an entirely subjective judgement. Parents who described their child as a 'maths genius' or a 'future Naomi Campbell' often seemed to base their assessment of their child's abilities on their own expectations of success, rather than on more generally recognised criteria of what constitutes genius or star quality. Parents who simply asserted that their children were 'special' because 'all children are special' often presented a more sympathetic account of their decision-making. For other children in the research, 'specialness' became understood in slightly more problematic ways; such as being culturally or religiously very different to the majority population. The identification of 'specialness' or 'otherness' often problematised educational expectations with many parents feeling their personal insight into their children's abilities and characteristics made them better able to determine what sort of education was most appropriate for them. Such decisions were often made against a backdrop in which schools were characterised as not recognising or adapting to the individual needs of their children. These same dilemmas and challenges were specifically noted by parents whose children were identified as having Special Educational Needs (SEN).

There is evidence that parents of children with disabilities and Special Educational Needs often believe they are better able to adapt individualised forms of

84 *Special educational needs and disability*

learning and teaching that take account of the medical needs of their children (Arora, 2006; Duvall, 2005; Collom, 2005; Lyman, 2000). At the same time many parents also identify specific failures of schools to meet their children's needs. A BBC investigation documented a 57% increase in the numbers of parents home educating their children with SEN almost entirely driven by concerns that schools were not meeting their needs (Jeffreys, 2015). In our research both of these accounts tended to play out simultaneously. For families whose children have a disability, the decision to home educate can be a complicated process not simply because of the practicalities of organising a programme of education. For such families the decision is one that also engages with societal expectations around disability. At a very fundamental level it opens up debates about medical or social approaches to disability. Some parents possibly choose an overtly medicalised approach on behalf of their children or an approach which prioritises responses to a medicalised condition rather than one that requires society to adapt to the needs of the child. In many respects the choice to home educate *because* of a child's disability also pushes against mainstream discourses which promote the movement towards more 'inclusive' schools in which children with disabilities 'integrate' in educational settings with non-disabled peers. This preference for inclusivity is well established globally and is essentially embodied within United Nations Convention on the Rights of the Child (United Nations, 1989) which has been ratified by nearly 200 countries (though not by the United States). In the UK policy has addressed this issue by requiring schools to be more inclusive, by identifying and providing additional support through Special Educational Needs statements for individual pupils with disabilities (Equality Act, 2010; DfE, 2014). It is also an approach that assumes schooling and/or education should be specifically adapted to an individual's set of circumstances. Overwhelmingly parents reported that schools were not delivering on these sorts of expectations. Their experience of mainstream education was of schools which often appeared to resent the adaptations required for their children.

Both the case studies in this chapter examine family choices based around responding to the needs of children with medically identifiable conditions. Both families could have chosen to remain within state schooling but concluded that it was within their child's interests to receive an education more specifically focused on their needs. Whilst there are many reasons for parents choosing home education, Houston argues that if 'schools are unable to deliver a product that is valued by the household because of the prevalence of negative environmental factors then the household will seek out alternative forms of education' (Houston, 1999: 86). This is particularly evident in the experiences of families whose children have SEN.

In the UK children with disabilities will normally have an official statement of SEN provided by their local education authority. This should form the basis for the local education authority ensuring that the needs of the child are met. Arora (2006) notes that parents who homeschool children with SEN feel that their needs can be accommodated better and more effectively at home, rather than at school because teaching, 'children with special needs is often seen as

Special educational needs and disability 85

requiring even more expertise than teaching a class of average learners' (Arora, 2006: 57). Arora (2006) argues that when parents are homeschooling children with SEN, local education authorities should provide adequate support for the child and their family, in order that a flexible education plan can be developed. Ideally this should include giving parents the opportunity to discuss different options of home education with a qualified SEN teacher with specialist practitioner skills; visits from teachers to assess their child's progress and telephone support for advice on teaching children who have specific special educational needs. There are however no current arrangements in place requiring local authorities to maintain working relationships with any home educating family. Home education is in many ways seen as constituting a break between the family and school that is marked by the cessation of state funding in the child's education, and also often characterised by home educating families, as a moment when the state ceases to interfere in their lives. The advocacy of home education groups that the state should not interfere in home educators' lives is perhaps a significant factor here that works against the interests of some families. In a context of austerity, budget pressures and schools increasingly engaging in the commodified markets that measure success in terms of both league tables and profit and loss accounts, the special may simply be identified as different, freighted with more expensive needs and leading to less successful measurable outcomes. In these sorts of markets there is little economic pressure to pull parents of children with SEN back into the mainstream if they choose to leave. Such a pattern also seemingly materialises in the often muted responses of schools and local authorities towards increasing numbers of pupils with 'difficult' histories of school attendance who are excluded.

The Wilson family

Mr and Mrs Wilson have two children; their son Matthew aged 10 who attends primary school and their daughter Lorna aged 13 who is currently home educated. Lorna attended primary school until she was 9 years old but the Wilsons withdrew her from school in year 5. She was home educated for the last two years of her primary school education and did not make the transition to secondary school aged 11.

The Wilsons live in a suburban town within the M25. Both parents grew up in West London and the decision to move away coincided with the birth of their second child; it was a move described by both parents as 'the best decision we ever made'. The family has lived in the same three bedroom semi-detached house ever since. They live in walking distance of shops, public transport links, leisure facilities and local schools. Mr Wilson works for the local council as a planning officer and in the past Mrs Wilson also worked part-time for the local council as an administrative officer.

The town is very mixed in terms of social class, reflected in the mix of different housing on adjacent streets. It is also very mixed in terms of the ethnic and religious backgrounds of residents; this features heavily in the local authorities'

86   *Special educational needs and disability*

portrayal of the town as a modern, multicultural and a forward-looking place to live. In addition to non-denominational schools there are also both Church of England and Catholic primary schools in the area; all of these have been graded either 'good' or 'outstanding' by OFSTED. The town is served by three secondary schools, one large co-educational academy and two smaller boys' and girls' schools. All three schools were assessed as being 'good' by OFSTED. The primary school currently attended by Matthew and previously by Lorna was graded 'good'.

The Wilsons explained that they had made the decision to home educate Lorna because she was dyslexic and they felt that the school did not address her specific needs. Mrs Wilson described the first time she felt that Lorna had some kind of problem with her reading and writing.

> I remember back when Lorna was in year 2 when she found it very difficult to recognise the letters and also kept getting them mixed up all the time. I didn't think much of it at the time, and looking back I thought it was just the normal learning process for her, so then I didn't bring it up. Then when she was in year 3 she kept making all the same mistakes and what was interesting was that it wasn't even picked up by the teachers. I decided to mention it to her teacher, who didn't seem to think there was a problem at all and in some ways kept saying it was normal. But there were other children who I didn't think were as bright as Lorna who were not having this problem. I then mentioned this to a friend of mine who is a teacher and she mentioned dyslexia.

Having identified the possibility that Lorna was struggling because she was dyslexic, the Wilsons decided to speak to her teacher to discuss what extra help might be available. Mrs Wilson spoke to Lorna's teacher in the first instance and later had an appointment with the deputy head to discuss their concerns, but found the school unhelpful.

> I was not very happy when the teacher questioned me and more or less said that I was overreacting, then when I asked to see the head teacher who asked another teacher to assess the situation, I was told the school would then think about getting Lorna tested to see if she was dyslexic and then statemented.

Mr Wilson described how the school always 'put on their most sympathetic face' when the family approached them but that this did not result in any 'actual, positive action'. Mrs Wilson described how her daughter was assigned extra one-to-one sessions with teaching assistants to help her with her reading, but that the school was unwilling to have an assessment made for dyslexia. The Wilsons suggested that although the school was graded as 'good' by OFSTED, it had very low numbers of children who were defined as having 'special

Special educational needs and disability 87

educational needs'. They felt this was indicative of both the school not wishing to engage with children who demonstrated special needs and also with a lack of experience on the part of the school. The family characterised the school as providing little provision or support for children with SEN. This was not however borne out in the school's most recent OFSTED report which highlighted the school's special educational needs provision as a particular strength of the school.

Mrs Wilson described her frustration at the school's unwillingness to respond to their request for Lorna to be assessed for dyslexia. She felt she had to instigate the identification of her child's special need, when it should have been the teachers who identified the problems and put in place teaching strategies to address these. In the end Mr and Mrs Wilson made arrangements for an educational psychologist to conduct a private assessment of Lorna which confirmed the family's diagnosis that she was dyslexic.

> It all took a very long time and in the end I had to fight for the statement and the extra help and the school weren't interested at all. We decided we would just go and do it ourselves because it was taking such a long time and I was at the point that I wanted to just know. Each day that we didn't know, we couldn't deal with it and do anything about it. If we left it to the school, we would have waited for another year – I am convinced of that. So we just went ahead ourselves and paid for a private assessment.

Mrs Wilson in particular described how she felt very let down by the school. She contextualised Lorna's experiences in terms of the school having responsibility for the needs of all its children and suggested the school overlooked educational disabilities such as dyslexia,

> If Lorna was physically disabled in some way, if she couldn't walk they would deal with that immediately. It is something they can see and they have evidence for it and so they act on it. Being dyslexic is not something that is obvious, it is something that has to be assessed and that some people may disagree with.

Mrs Wilson was upset that going to school did not necessarily mean that all children are included in the same ways.

> I believe that schools have a duty to include all children in their learning experiences and some schools say that and our primary school said that. But, when it came to the individual case of our child, that was not the case and it was like the school did not want to deal with it – because it would create too many problems. So instead of doing what they had to do to include Lorna it was the reverse. She was being excluded and in some ways punished because she has a special need.

88   *Special educational needs and disability*

Mrs Wilson also felt that this contributed to the school not being proactive in addressing her daughter's need; and, as a consequence, the responsibility for taking the initiative fell back to the family.

> The schools have to ensure that they are looking after all the children and they have to listen to the needs of parents. This does not happen, it is usually those problems that are obvious that are dealt with and those parents who are able to shout the loudest.

Mrs Wilson described her family as being from a middle-class background and suggested they were 'comfortably off'. Both parents had been to university and they were both well spoken.

> Even parents like us who are able to be confident enough to go to the school and demand to see the head teacher expect them to listen to us. But this did not happen. I worry about those parents who don't feel confident about going to the school to raise an issue and those children who have got special needs who are slipping through the net. These kinds of problems have to be picked up quickly otherwise it can be too late to address them.

Following the diagnosis by the educational psychologist, the Wilsons anticipated the school would provide greater support for Lorna in the classroom but felt this was not forthcoming. Following discussions with the special educational needs coordinator (SENCO), they were told the school would continue to offer the additional one-to-one sessions to help with Lorna's reading and that the school would also carry out some observations on Lorna. According to the Wilsons, this moment was a tipping point for them personally as they believed the school should be offering more support. Mr Wilson suggested:

> I felt they were worse than useless. We met the special needs teacher and all he could come up with was some coloured plastic screens and that in class they were using a screen with different coloured writing on. It felt like we were dealing with a school in the stone age. I had a big falling out with the headmistress.

The Wilsons felt they had worked hard to get support for Lorna but that the school either delayed or failed to deliver on her specific needs. When asked what sort of support would have been effective for Lorna, the Wilsons suggested she needed a mix of speech and musical therapy tailored to her individual skills; and, that the school should have investigated the possibilities for 'assistive technologies' that could be used in the classroom by Lorna. They felt the primary school tended to suggest Lorna should simply adapt to its daily routines, with the expectation that a more tailored approach to her learning would become a reality at secondary school. When asked whether the family's

Special educational needs and disability 89

perspective of what the school should offer was realistic and whether the school might also have some expertise to offer Mr Wilson said:

> It's realistic that we want the best for our children. The school were never interested in that and I understand that. They have hundreds of children to teach but we just have one. And we know that one child needs the very best.

Asked about Lorna's younger brother, Matthew's experiences at the school, Mrs Wilson said:

> He's very different. You just know he's going to be one of those straight A kids who never look back. I was worried when everything was going on around Lorna that they would backfire on Matt but they haven't. The school is great with him.

Shortly after the beginning of year 5, the Wilsons withdrew Lorna from school to be home educated by Mrs Wilson. For two years Mrs Wilson implemented a fairly rigorous routine in which she and Lorna worked on maths and English in the mornings, but with afternoons set aside for more 'fun' activities including museum visits, walks and swimming. The family also invested heavily in music and singing lessons for Lorna. The Wilsons described the dilemma they had when Lorna was 11 years old and could potentially start secondary school. Despite visiting local secondary schools, the family chose to continue home educating, according to Mrs Wilson.

> I don't have the confidence in the schools. Lorna is doing so well now. But that comes down to her getting all the attention she needs. That's not what schools have to offer. We have such a close bond. I would do the same for Matthew but he's like 'mum, no way, I'm going to school'. They are very different and you need to recognise that.

Having made the decision to home educate, Mrs Wilson contacted her local authority to let them know that she was home educating and asked them for the support that was available. The information for Mrs Wilson's local authority states,

> Parents are allowed to educate their children at home instead of school if they choose to do so. Under English law, it is education that is compulsory, not schooling, though the vast majority of parents do choose to send their children to school. There are no funds directly available for parents who decide to home educate their children. Local authorities have no legal duty to provide financial support to parents who choose to home educate their children. However, some local authorities do provide free national curriculum materials and other support to parents. The level and extent of

90 *Special educational needs and disability*

such support is decided locally, based on the local authority's own policies and the needs of the child.

(Council guidelines on home education, accessed November 2015)

Although the Wilsons concluded from this that they would receive little support from their local authority, Mrs Wilson described her shock at how little information they were able to provide:

> I didn't get much help from the local authority, they said there were no national guidelines only the guidelines they had which said I can home educate and that was it. They were unable to give me any guidance on curriculum and just directed me to the Department of Education websites which have information on the curriculum. They also gave me some names of organisations who support home educators, but that was it to be honest.

Mrs Wilson spoke about the reaction she received from her local school and also the local education authority when she told them she had decided to home educate.

> I think the school were shocked when I told them I was going to take Lorna out of school to home educate her. I did say to them that I was not very happy with the way the school had dealt with her special need. I think they have not had many parents who make this decision so were shocked by it. The (local authority) were not very helpful and did not really provide me with any support, again I think there are not many families who make this decision.

Mrs Wilson carried out her own research on the different types of support available to home educators and in this process accessed websites dedicated to home education. In addition to joining a local support group she also actively engages with an organisation that offers

> lots of support for children who have special needs and how those needs can be catered for and addressed. We suddenly realised there are actually a lot of other families just like us.

Mrs Wilson spoke about the support she received from other parents and the importance of the support that Lorna received from other children who were being home educated. She and Lorna had attended a variety of different groups set up by home educators. One support group that met locally every week for home-educating parents was mostly organised around families with primary school-aged children and later a smaller offshoot had emerged around two or three families with older children. In addition Mrs Wilson was connected to several groups that catered either for home educators of dyslexic children

Special educational needs and disability 91

specifically or children with disabilities more generally. These were largely internet-based, though meetings and family days out were arranged through these groups. Most importantly for Mrs Wilson was the opportunity to build a wider social network around parents with other similar circumstances.

> We meet once a week if we can with other parents in the area who are home educating. We found out about this when we joined (local home education support group) and so we make an effort to meet up with them. The once a week meetings happen all the time, but there are other times that we meet with some of the families. The one thing that I like about meeting with the parents and the children is that Lorna is just like another child. She isn't treated as the one who needs help and who is dyslexic – she is treated as another child who is home educated. She is included with everyone else, at school she was excluded and there was more scope for her to be excluded.

Mrs Wilson was able to discuss her experiences of home education and was reassured that she was not the only parent who was dissatisfied with the way the school treated Lorna. She described how most other parents whose children had different special educational needs did not feel entirely satisfied with their school experiences. The overall picture she painted was of little understanding of the individual needs of pupils who had SEN, and far more emphasis placed on the bureaucracy surrounding a child being officially given a statement of SEN. Mrs Wilson emphasised that whilst there were some schools who were truly inclusive, this was not her experience or indeed other parents who were home educating.

> When you have a child who is labelled as having special educational needs, that label in schools sticks with them and will stay with them for a long time. The school that Lorna went to were unable to provide the support we needed but at the same time the label of her being a child who had special needs would have stayed with her forever and that would affect her progress and her confidence. Being home educated, that does not happen. All the children are treated as children and as individuals and not labelled as children with having this or that special need and that makes a difference to their experience.

Mrs Wilson felt she had made the right decision for Lorna to be home educated because she felt that her experience at school was not being addressed and that highlighting Lorna's problem only worked towards exacerbating the situation and labelling Lorna which would affect her future educational choices and options.

One of the ironies that seemed to fill the Wilsons' account was the seemingly contradictory emphasis on both the need for her to receive an individualised learning package catering specifically to her personal needs, and also, the suggestion that she should be treated just like everyone else. Whilst

92 *Special educational needs and disability*

this was primarily identified by Mrs Wilson (who was by far the most vocal participant in the interviews), it was also succinctly endorsed by Mr Wilson who suggested

> Treating people fairly means recognising how they are different. Being fair is about levelling things up. It makes me angry that both my children go to the same school but only one of them seems to do well there.

The family used home education to manage concerns they identified in their children's education and future prospects. In many ways the prospect that their younger son was doing well at school seemed to be a significant factor in identifying the risks associated with Lorna's education. In some respects this reflected the earlier concerns raised by the family when comparing Lorna to her peers and the identification that she was doing less well at school. Whilst the school was repeatedly portrayed as 'doing nothing' this was not entirely accurate; the Wilson's described in some detail the additional resources given over to Lorna's schooling, including extra one-to-one teaching and the school's adoption (prior to Lorna being identified as dyslexic) of classroom reading aids. Rather, what appeared to stand out in the Wilsons' account was the feeling that the type of tailored education on offer from the school was not the type of education the Wilsons personally identified as being suitable. Like many other families in this research, the Wilsons noted the long time it took to be diagnosed and for specific actions to be put in place around their daughter and this clearly influenced their assessment of the school's professionalism and expertise. The early negative shaping of these judgements also impacted upon the later relationship that developed between the school and family. The family felt there was a need to personally manage the risks they identified in Lorna's education and which Mr Wilson again very succinctly placed within an understanding of education in an era of neo-liberalism.

> It's our choice. We can make Lorna's future better if the school won't do that. Other families are not interested but we're not other families. We can make choices and we can change things for us.

The emphasis on choice and creating future security for the family suggested they were assessing the risks and dangers that the future held and developing strategies to manage these individually. In this context the school had possibilities of usefulness; it was for example identified as a useful and positive experience for Matthew to attend school and his future prospects were identified as benefitting from attendance. The family appeared to identify that Lorna's attendance at school related to less effective outcomes. In Lorna's case this was directly related to the identification of her disability; however in a more wide-ranging discussion of home education, the Wilsons entered into an interesting exchange about our research. Mrs Wilson had asked about other families and whether we were mostly interested in children with different disabilities, to

Special educational needs and disability 93

which the interviewer had explained that the research was looking at all sorts of different families, including different religious and ethnic backgrounds:

Mrs Wilson: I know in [local home education support group] we have a mix. [A family friend who is home educating] is because her girl is so little . . . she's 8 but everyone thinks she's in reception. The twins [two home educated children who were close friends of Lorna] are doing it because they need to spend more time on their dance. They've been on TV.

Mr Wilson: They do advertising work. They make money though. Quite serious money. Lots of people do that.

Interviewer: When I first found out about home education it was Gypsy families. They often home educate.

Mr Wilson: Work again. Gypsy boys do better if they learn skills. That's what it comes down to. I've a lot of time for them. Gypsies. We use them on the sites [building sites that Mr Wilson was responsible for]. If they go to school everyone hates them and they end up useless. They teach themselves and they make good money. You can't just rely on schools.

Mrs Wilson: Well we don't do we?

In many respects the Wilsons possessed both an optimistic and opportunistic view of the world. They identified difficulties that would impact upon their children's lives but actively worked to adapt around these. At face value, the choices made for Lorna did not sit comfortably with widely held expectations of a successful transition from education into the employment market; it was however clear that the Wilsons were managing and responding to difficulties in her life.

The Knight family

Mr and Mrs Knight have three children, Edward is 8, Joe is 6 and Julie is 5. The Knights live in a suburban town in the south-east of England. It is an area that has been subject to significant development for over 20 years and this is reflected in the large housing estates that now fill what used to be agricultural land, networks of new roads, shopping and leisure facilities. The area has also seen a progressive redevelopment of its schools (both primary and secondary) since the 1990s – most of which are characterised by new buildings. Despite this growth, the town centre retains a distinct identity and presents an image that it is thriving. Mr and Mrs Knight sent all their children to their local primary school which is a 10-minute walk from their house.

This school is popular and has a very good reputation locally. The school was graded as being 'good' by OFSTED which compares unfavourably with two proximate schools both of which were rated as 'outstanding'. Parents at the school however often highlight the school's reputation for inclusivity,

94 *Special educational needs and disability*

particularly for pupils with physical disabilities. The Knights described how one of the nearby 'outstanding' schools was regarded as being 'too posh' and the other school was too far away. Both the Knights grew up in the area and Mr Knight attended the same primary school himself when he was growing up, although in the intervening years the school buildings were demolished and rebuilt to accommodate a greater school intake. According to the Knights, the school had benefited from the appointment of a new and excellent head teacher 6 years previously.

Whilst the school serves a community drawn from a fairly narrow geographical area, its pupil population represents a very diverse mixture of families compared to other local schools, reflecting the local demographics. There are significant numbers of families reliant on state benefits and families whose children are eligible for free school meals, as well as many families from professional and semi-professional backgrounds. The streets immediately adjacent to the school include social housing, smaller newer build properties that are both owner occupied and housing association stock, and also, streets with more substantial, older detached properties. The local area and the town has a predominantly White population; however the school itself has higher than average numbers of Black and minority ethnic pupils (though these numbers are still comparatively small), and a small number of East European pupils.

Whilst the proportion of children who are supported with SEN is below the national average, the school seems very clear about its inclusive ethos. The school's website includes clear guidance to its own inclusion policies and also signposts parents to named teachers who can assist parents concerned about SEN issues. In addition, the website provides links to a range of other useful sites (both government and charitable), related to specific disabilities. The school recently refurbished space within the school as an on-site unit adapted around the specific needs of four pupils with physical disabilities. Amongst the previous year's school newsletters was an account of a week spent by final year pupils at an out-of-bounds centre disrupted by appalling weather, in which the experiences of one child in a motorised wheelchair were included.

The Knights became concerned that Edward was not doing as well at school as they hoped when he was aged 6. Mrs Knight noticed that Edward was finding it difficult to concentrate at school and was starting to get into trouble at school because of his behaviour.

> I did notice that Edward was getting more and more anxious at school and that he was getting into trouble more. The teachers spoke to me about it various times, saying that he was not behaving properly towards the other children. He was coming across as a bit aggressive and I wasn't clear where that was coming from. One day, he pushed another pupil and threatened to spit in his face. I was very worried but at that time didn't think there was anything that was wrong with him, I wondered whether there was someone at school he was reacting against.

Mrs Knight spoke to Edward's classroom teacher on a number occasions around this time both in response to specific instances where there had been a problem during the school day and also more generally to discuss his progress. Mrs Knight recalled having conversations about whether or not Edward's behaviour was just him being a 'naughty child' who had difficulties adhering to the rules and the expected behaviour of children in the classroom, or whether there were other underlying causes.

> When I first spoke to the teachers, they didn't mention anything about Edward having any kind of real problems or special educational needs. So we had these conversations about what sort of boy was Edward. Was he a naughty boy? What was he like at home? Was he naughty at home? How did he get on with the two younger ones? Was everything alright at home? Was there something that might be upsetting him and making him upset at school. I know they were trying to see all the different angles but I came away feeling terrible. I lost a lot of faith in the school and the teachers.

Despite this, the Knights continued to talk with the school on a regular basis. Mr Knight explained how he would leave work early so that they could both pick Edward up from school and talk to his classroom teacher and to the school's Special Educational Needs Coordinator.

> I felt the school were a little bit too hands off for too long. But then they would say they didn't want to pre-judge the situation. It was the SENCO teacher who first mentioned autism to us. But it was never made clear what the school was or was not doing. In the beginning I thought they were useless. And I felt we were useless. Neither of us knew what to do and I think it all became very tense.

Mr Knight's description of a lack of action on the part of the school and the family belied a very active approach that was actually taken by everyone concerned. The Knights approached their GP for advice and Edward was diagnosed with autism, they searched out information on the internet and local library and contacted a number of organisations and charities who supported people with autism. The school was proactive in making arrangements to negotiate with the local authority for some additional resources (a small number of hours from a teaching assistant). The SENCO and Edward's teacher identified strategies to help Edward's learning. In some respects the process of being 'officially' diagnosed with a moderate form of autism meant both the school and the family were able to move forward, according to Mr Knight.

> It seemed to take too long but after the diagnosis everyone seemed to be much more together. I think we knew what we were doing and the school knew what they were doing. The other thing was that Joe (the family's middle son) had started school and it was only then that we realised how

96   *Special educational needs and disability*

much easier it was for him. I think we weren't aware that Edward was having such a hard time. Because he was the first child it was almost as though that was normal.

The experience of having other children at the school (the Knight's daughter Julie moved from reception to year 1 a year after Joe), had a dramatic impact on the parent's feelings about school. Mrs Knight described how her concerns grew.

I went to speak to Julie's teacher about three weeks after she had started in year one. They ask all the new parents in to have a chat and make sure everything is OK. I made a joke about not having really said 'hello' to the teacher and I think then it came home to me how much time and pressure there was around Edward. I got very teary. I suddenly felt how did we get here?

Mrs Knight went on to explain how whilst Edward seemed happier at school with the additional support, there were still problems. In particular Edward was often very insular and did not really talk with other children in his class. Whilst Mrs Knight did not believe this had worsened over time, she felt it had become much more noticeable to other children in the class. She highlighted that as the children became older they tended to notice more things around them (including her son's behaviour), but also that the extra time spent with teaching assistants made Edward stand out as being different from his peers. She also felt that again whilst the problems associated with Edward's autism remained a constant and did not worsen, the response to them changed as the other children got older. She described how some of Edwards' behavioural problems towards other children continued and this had brought her into conflict with other parents. She noted that the school was always very good at negotiating these relationships after there had been an incident, but felt that some other parents were uncomfortable around her. She also described how other children had begun to bully Edward because of his social behaviour. Again she noted that the school was effective at managing these incidents after they happened, but she was increasingly worried about the impact they would have on Edward. As a result Mrs Knight began to think about other options for Edward's education and suggested to her husband that they should take him out of school. Mr Knight explained how this caused a lot of friction between them.

I went mad. I thought after all this time everything's settled and now you're not happy. I was mad at the school before, but to be fair they had worked really hard and now we take him out of school? Really? So we ended up having a very long conversation.

Mrs Knight had remained quite adamant that the school was no longer the best option for Edward's education and therefore the family needed to think about alternative choices. The Knights had already visited a special school run by the local authority which catered for some pupils with learning difficulties, but

Special educational needs and disability 97

were not convinced it was a good option for them, as the family would need to rely on the school's bus which picked children up early and brought them home quite late in the day. In addition Mrs Knight suggested that,

> I thought maybe Edward would end up going to [the special school] when he was older. I don't see him attending secondary school. And I didn't want that to be his whole school life somehow. It's a great place but it's full of kids like Edward.

Mrs Knight suggested to her husband that they should think about home education for Edward but Mr Knight was resolutely opposed to the idea.

> I was dead set against it. We're not teachers. I said to [Mrs Knight] I don't think you can do this. You can't just teach.

Mrs Knight however remained convinced that it would be better for Edward to be home educated. She felt that she and her husband had continually failed to recognise how difficult Edward's experience of schooling had been. In particular she characterised his experience of learning and interactions with other pupils and the teachers as being very poor. Despite recognising that the school was doing much to support Edward's needs, she felt he was just one child in a classroom of 32 children, all of whose needs that had to be catered for and addressed.

> I thought long and hard about taking Edward out of school and educating him at home for many different reasons. I am not that educated myself. I did not go to university for example and I don't know that much about the curriculum. But then I could see how much he was struggling not just with his behaviour but also with his learning I just felt I could do better than this. He could be at home with me and I could just teach him and he would have all my attention. I wasn't working anyway. I have been at home with the children since Edward was born so it wouldn't have made much difference to me as I am at home anyway and we were not going to lose a salary.

Despite Mr Knight feeling it was the wrong decision, the Knights agreed that Edward would be home educated. Mr Knight suggested that this decision was only agreed with a number of provisos and following discussions with the local authority and school. The family had agreed with the local authority that if home education was an unsuccessful choice, then Edward could return to his original primary school. The local authority had suggested that in many respects this was not a concession to the family, but reflected their general practice given Edward and his family's circumstances. However, both Mr and Mrs Knight noted the importance they attached to this agreement. In the short term the school had suggested that Edward could attend school on

98   *Special educational needs and disability*

a part-time basis; possibly attending school for two or three days a week and being home educated for the remaining days. The Knights had not taken up this offer but had agreed that in principle it might be a useful option in the future. Mrs Knight had also agreed with Mr Knight that if Edward suggested he wanted to return to school, then that would have to be the family's decision. Both parents also suggested that the decision to home educate was probably a short-term strategy and that in the future they would have to consider other options: either sending Edward to the local authority-run special school or possibly making arrangements to attend a non-maintained school run by a charity.

Reflecting on her experience of home educating Edward for just over a year Mrs Knight said,

> I feel it was the best decision. I was so stressed and now we are a lot calmer. Joe and Julie are very settled at school. Edward is Edward. I think he's happier.

Mrs Knight carried out a lot of research on home education and exploring some of the challenges that children with autism face. She contacted various home education organisations who put her in touch with organisations who had experts on autism and special educational needs, as well as with families who were home educating, some of whom were themselves educating children with special educational needs.

> The support I received from [home education organisation] was excellent. When I told them that I was home educating a child who had special needs, they gave me lots of different information and also put me in touch with other families. They are very good and knowledgeable about home education, for instance I had no idea that I didn't have to stick to the curriculum I assumed that I would have to teach Edward everything in the curriculum and that makes it much easier for me.

Having home educated Edward for two years, Mrs Knight felt his learning had increased and she could see the difference in his behaviour. She did not regret home educating him, but did worry about his future.

> I am not sure if we are going to continue to home educate Edward when he reaches secondary school age that is something that I need to think about. I will cross that bridge when I have to, but I am happy to continue at the moment.

In many respects home education did not resolve the Knights' concerns. They had very specific concerns about Edward's school attendance which were perhaps resolved by not attending school but their wider concerns about how he should be educated were to a large extent unanswered. The significant decisions about where and how he would be educated when he reached secondary school age were effectively (and understandably) postponed by the family.

Conclusions

This chapter has explored two case studies on families with children who have been identified as having SEN. There were a number of striking differences between the Wilsons and the Knights. Not least was a difference in approach to demarcations of where responsibilities should lie for schools and parents. The Wilsons followed a much clearer path; from identifying that the school was not delivering the type of education they believed was best for Lorna, to a position of the family taking over responsibility and determining what sort of education was appropriate. The Knights, on the other hand, having identified failings in the school's provision of education, still identified schooling as a preferred, though to date inadequate, route to education. The two families' different approaches perhaps in some ways exemplify the difficulties associated with addressing social changes of late modernity. For families like the Knights, there is a sense in which they are stranded by under-resourced schools whose priorities are not those of their children. The promises of successive governments of a universal education for all children were not being met. The decision to home educate was effectively one that was forced upon them; their management of risk was not being shaped by them acting as free agents making choices within a free-market economy. Instead home education was the family's only option. By contrast the Wilsons, faced with similar difficulties, seemed more adept at conceptualising the failure of schools to address their personal needs as an everyday part of life. They were unhappy that the school was in their eyes letting their daughter down, but seemed to readily comprehend this was simply one issue that could be resolved by adopting alternative strategies to educate their daughter. They seemed genuinely representative of a family making consumer-type choices about education in a neo-liberal setting.

Whilst the distinction in conceptualising the issues was apparent between the two families, what seemed a lot less clear was how effective their decision to home educate would be for their children. Arguably neither family appeared well positioned to provide their children with all the skills and knowledge that would hopefully have been learned at school. The reliance on home-educating organisations and local support groups was something that many families, not just those whose children had special needs, often cited as being of great importance to their children's progress. The engagement with these groups was important in establishing the evidence that the decision to home educate was a good one, meeting like-minded people and validating what were often difficult decisions. Amongst families whose children had disabilities, often the support groups included the sharing of similar experiences of difficulties, such as having disability recognised by schools, or of adequate responses to individual children's needs. For many parents accessing a network of sympathetic and like-minded other parents was a very welcome experience.

A similar bonding and sharing of experience could be seen to have a wider resonance with the identification of children as being 'special' or 'gifted'. The Wilsons for example commented how the members of a local support group

100 *Special educational needs and disability*

were very different but that all shared particular traits of individuality; be that they had a disability or that they were particularly 'gifted'. Such individuality was identified as being problematic for schools that were faced with the need to educate lots of similar children rather than specific individuals. The identification of 'specialness' was noticeable throughout the research though often articulated in different ways by different families related to class or ethnicity.

The identification of 'specialness' by home educators may be equated to spatial and emotional geographies 'that characterise homeschoolers' experiences, where feelings of intimacy and love are, in large measure, constitutive of what makes homeschooling an 'alternative' space to mainstream schools' (Kraftl, 2013). The identification of such family intimacy was apparent in some of the descriptions of parents home educating disabled children, but was also noticeably not an overriding concern. The Wilsons for example made a clear connection between the security and emotional support of a home education for their dyslexic child but did not mirror this in their approach more generally to accommodate their non-disabled child. 'Risk' was identified as being specific to the disability and therefore to a requirement for personal, family management; their other child, a 'straight A' pupil, doing well with all the other children at school, was allowed to engage in a more social, less intimate social life. This parallels Neuman and Aviram's (2003) discussion of home education as a problem-solving measure in which problems associated with earlier family experiences or the child's current schooling can be resolved within the family. What was striking in the Wilsons' account was the identification that the child without a disability was therefore quite capable of engaging in mainstream education, in many respects reflecting a consumer-orientated choice. There was never any indication that the family valued one child more or less than the other; they did however identify different risks or problems to be resolved by the family.

The linking of specialness to the need for closer family engagement was a persistent feature of families who identified their child as having a special talent that was not fully appreciated or supported by mainstream schools. So for example the mother of two daughters who were 'musically gifted' was very proud to demonstrate a home environment entirely given over to the celebration of her daughters' successes. The walls of her house were covered in certificates of achievement in musical instruments, photographs of performances and newspaper coverage of local shows her daughters had participated in. For this family, the home materialised as a space created around the identity of her children delineated solely by their special gifts.

The two case studies demonstrate the frustration and challenges that parents with children who have special educational needs often face. They struggle to get teachers to understand the specific needs of their children; the processes of agreeing statements of SEN and getting extra help can all be time consuming and emotionally draining. Parents felt their children would be better educated at home because they could cater to the needs of their children, rather than their children competing in large classrooms for the attention of the teacher. Parents also felt that whilst academic success was important, learning social skills and

Special educational needs and disability   101

children mixing with others was crucial to their well-being and development. Consequently, the support that families received via home education organisations and other organisations that had knowledge of special needs was vital in their decisions to home educate. Whilst home educating a child with special educational needs was different to educating a child without special educational needs, many home-educating families described very similar processes in their decision-making. Parents stressed their awareness of catering for the individual needs of their child, but at the same time recognising wider measures of learning and development. Traditional curriculum materials were generally available from home education organisations and in some cases families were supported to access these by local authorities; but, as was the case generally for home educating families, there was little pressure to adopt or prioritise these as learning materials. Addressing and understanding the specific or special educational needs identified with their children were generally considered a priority.

8 Race and ethnicity

Local, global or cosmopolitan identities?

Black and Asian families who participated in the research often discussed issues about their children's education that mirrored those of a wide range of families. They identified the same fears as many other parents about the effectiveness of local schools and expressed similar views about the importance of providing their children with opportunities to secure the best possible outcomes in later life. In many respects the decisions made by Black middle-class families to home educate were shaped by the same concerns as other middle-class families and by their access to similar resources. However, all the Black and Asian families who participated in the research also specifically made reference to experiencing racism directly or being concerned that race would have a detrimental effect on their child's educational experiences. This chapter explores these specific concerns and suggests that in urban settings in particular, for identities shaped by race, racism and global family histories, alternative approaches to education become identified as an effective strategy. In twenty-first century educational markets if one product fails, the market may look to fill the gap with a new product; one of the features of home education in the UK is how it is often a highly individualised or personal means to occupy such gaps.

Discussion of the impact of race and racism are also addressed in previous chapters in relation to Gypsy and Traveller families (Chapter 5) and Asian Muslims (Chapter 6). This chapter continues that discussion both by looking at the experiences of two families who accessed or considered a range of alternatives to mainstream schooling including, but not limited to homeschooling. Both families identified themselves in part as being both British and Black; however they also identified a wider heritage related to family routes from Africa and the Caribbean. Their family histories also included the impact of parents changing partners and of children being identified as mixed race.

This chapter also highlights two families whose experience of home education differs somewhat to the experiences of families in other chapters. The most significant difference being The Woods' decision *not to home educate*. Despite seriously considering home education as a potential strategy to address problems the family identified in their dealings with local schools, and, at the time of the research the family still considered home education as a potential option, they chose not to go ahead with this approach. Whilst putting in place

Race and ethnicity   103

alternative provisions to address the problems they faced, they identified home education as being a strategy they would prefer not to adopt. The second family discussed in this chapter also significantly differed to other families. They described circumstances in which they felt home education was forced upon them by the local education authority and school, believing they were *pushed into home education*. Risk in this latter case possibly represents the institutional management of risk associated with problematic parents. For the Alabis what emerged was a sense in which the institutional account of their 'global' or 'cosmopolitan' identity sat at odds with the school's templates for model students.

In many respects these families highlight Stuart Hall's (2003) descriptions of diasporic identities shaped by both 'belonging' and 'becoming' or of the distinction between an individual's 'roots' and 'routes'. In doing so they evidence Gilroy's (2002) account of acculturation, shaped by transnational or transcultural experiences, that often materialises in specifically local, urban contexts of resistance and protection of family culture and identity. This management of risks identified around schooling whilst mirroring the wider contexts of many home educators is differently shaped by family accounts of ethnicity and identity. Such acculturation processes also tended to describe identities that were fluid and not fixed by the completion of diasporic journeys; they were 'continuous, contested, negotiations that will forever be in progress as an immigrant grapples with his/her place in the larger structures of the history, culture, and politics' (Bhatia and Ram, 2009: 148). The importance of local, urban settings was apparent in both of these accounts, but also in many respects tended to undermine some of the anticipated cosmopolitanism that might inform Beck's notions of risk. Rather than stressing the global:local binaries, these families identified local risks shaped by local solutions in which their transnational identities appeared to materialise in specifically local contexts. In many respects they displayed a 'self-referential quality' (Beck et al., 2003) rather than a structural reflexivity towards modernity, a quality that might be associated with agency constructed in the local, everyday *minutiae* of decision-making. These accounts echo the ethical narrative understandings suggested by Ricoeur in which individual's 'fundamental potentialities' (Ricoeur, 1980: 183) drive events forwards. This is not to suggest these families distanced themselves from their *roots* or that their identities did not encompass significant understandings of cultural inheritance and heritage; rather they adapted them to personal dilemmas in the present.

The Woods family

The Woods family lived in North London. Melanie Wood had a 16-year-old daughter, Helena, and a 10-year-old son, Stevie, from a previous relationship. The children's biological father had died in a car accident whilst Melanie was pregnant with Stevie. Melanie described herself at different times as 'Trinidadian British', 'Black British', 'third-generation British' and 'British'. She was born in Britain but her parents, grandparents and extended family retained strong connections with Trinidad. She described Helena and Stevie's biological

104   *Race and ethnicity*

father as being, 'Black British but mixed. His mum was English. Is English. She's White.' After the death of the children's father she started a relationship with Rob who described himself as 'White. British. European . . . global citizen. Whatever really.'

Melanie and Rob had both grown up in the same locality and knew each other through extensive and longstanding, social networks of friends and family before entering into a relationship. According to Melanie they had first met at college when they were 16 years old. This was disputed by Rob who believes they previously attended the same primary school. Melanie described how the death of her partner and the children's father was the defining moment of the family.

> At the time I thought *that's it*. Everything. It's all over and there's never going to be a way back. Everything I could think about; Helena, being pregnant, my job, the flat, everything you thought about was not right anymore. None of it could stay the same. And it couldn't. Everything had to change and move on.

She described how she and Rob had begun a relationship 4 years later,

> I always say we were just so quiet. I knew it was difficult. And I knew that he knew it was going to be difficult. And Helena knew. We just had all these conversations going over all the same ground. I thought it was the wrong time. Rob thought it was the wrong time. It was always going to be wrong.

Melanie noted how following the death of the children's father she very quickly developed a network of people who she relied on. This initially included her parents who had only recently retired and returned to live in Trinidad, but who decided to return to the UK and move into their daughter's flat for just over a year. She recalled her father giving her very 'hard-boiled' advice that she valued about the need to toughen up, go back to work and provide security for her children. Melanie received support from her mother-in-law (the children's paternal grandmother), who regularly provided childcare and played a continuing role in her grandchildren's lives. Melanie's wider social networks of friends included Rob's family. Rob described the social events that tended to frame his daily life which included socialising and drinking with friends in local pubs and clubs; and also described how these often intersected with social functions around his own extended family or with the extended families of his friends. Melanie, her friends and her extended family were part of this wider network. Rob explained how, as his relationship with Melanie developed, he also began to make connections with her children (playing with them or taking them to football matches for example).

Four years after the death of the children's father, Melanie felt there was a degree of stability in her life. She was working part-time and beginning to consider the possibility of entering into a new relationship with Rob. Melanie

Race and ethnicity   105

described how at this moment she became aware that Helena, who was in Year 5 at primary school was unhappy.

> She seemed to go into herself. I understood but was caught out. When her dad died she was in shock, we all stopped really. But I think I felt Helena was the one who coped best. Stevie didn't know anything. I was wrecked. I just thought Helena would go to school. And she had her friends.

Melanie described how Jenny (Helena and Stevie's paternal grandmother) went to discuss their concerns with the school.

> Usually I would have gone but I was ill or something and Jenny went to speak to her teacher and she ended up talking to the head teacher as well. When she came back she was really angry and upset with the school. Really swearing. Which is so unlike her. Basically she said they were useless. Firstly, they didn't believe Jenny was their grandmother. The teacher ended up speaking to the head to confirm she was who she said she was. And secondly, the teacher didn't know anything about their dad being in a car crash. She was a new teacher that year but had never been told or had never found out that Helena was still in a very vulnerable place. Anyway. After that she explains how poorly Helena has been doing at school. How to all intents and purposes for two years her English and Maths have not been improving at all. And added on to all that she says Helena is quite disruptive. That she gets into fights with some boys. When Jenny asked her what the school was doing she was pretty much told there's nothing the school can do. That there are lots of disruptive children and their parents don't instil any discipline.

Melanie acknowledged that it was perhaps unsurprising a new teacher was unaware of the circumstances around the death of her daughter's father 4 years previously. However, she outlined a very detailed account of her understanding of the processes in which the school had failed to properly manage Helena's education. She argued that when Helena's behaviour significantly changed or became a concern, her teacher should respond to this both in her classroom practice and in communication with the home. If Helena was being disruptive or failing to progress, then in dealing with those issues, the classroom teacher would have been made aware of Helena's history. This would include discovering the circumstances around the death of Helena's father, which was well known within the school. This was an important factor that should have shaped the teacher's management of the situation. According to Melanie, none of this appeared to happen: Helena's teacher appeared to have almost no knowledge of her personal circumstances, she had not responded to a range of problematic behaviours and had made no effort to contact the home.

Melanie recalled being quite shocked by how angry Jenny was about the school's perceived failure and her surprise when she suggested it was related to

106 *Race and ethnicity*

race. She described how her own view of the school up until this moment had always been that it was a good and friendly school. Melanie described how she reflected on earlier conversations she had with the teacher,

> I remember she just made these very bland statements that everything was fine.

At this stage the school did appear to acknowledge Helena's teacher had been at fault and this was discussed at a number of meetings between Melanie, the Head teacher and the classroom teacher. Whilst the school seemed willing to put measures in place that would ensure Helena received closer attention and was taught in a more supportive fashion, her mother felt this was not necessarily enough. Melanie identified this moment as being the most important challenge since her partner had died, with all her energies being expended on dealing with her own and her daughter's grief, the challenges of a new baby and establishing workable new routines. In the process she felt she lost sight of new challenges or risks in her life such as whether or not her child's school was providing appropriate educational opportunities.

> It was another wake up call. Like my dad saying you need a job. You need security. I just thought Helena needs to do well. She needs an education and she needs a job. And what the school were doing wasn't enough.

Melanie described how she identified a number of options that could make a difference to Melanie's education. She did this primarily within discussions with Jenny and her own parents. She was surprised by her father's immediate response in which he suggested Melanie's own education had been restricted by 'white teachers who thought Black children were all failures'. Despite having very positive recollections of her own schooling (particularly primary school), Melanie began to question some of her experiences. Melanie had left school at 18 with three 'A' Levels but felt they were in non-academic subjects that in retrospect she would not choose and that she only just passed all three. Both her parents had ambitions for Melanie to attend university and pressured her to apply. She was offered a place at a local post-1992 university but decided not to take this up. This led to a temporary breakdown in relations with her father who felt she missed a very important opportunity in her life, and that now,

> He felt that history was repeating itself. That Helena would just coast through and no one make her fulfill her potential. He and mum started sending all these links to schools in Trinidad. They kept saying Helena could come and live there. Go to a good school. That I could go and live there and Stevie. Mad stuff really.

Other possibilities that were immediately identified were that Helena should change primary schools and have a fresh start with greater monitoring by the

Race and ethnicity 107

family of her education. Jenny identified the possibility of employing a tutor to help Helena in the short term to improve in Maths and English. However, Melanie concluded that all three of these individual solutions came encumbered with specific problems. Melanie ruled out being separated from Helena at all costs and was equally convinced that she did not want to move with the family to Trinidad. Her home and her social networks were all in North London, and although she had been to Trinidad many times in the past, it was not where she felt she had a future. She felt that moving Helena from primary school for just over one school year could prove unnecessarily disruptive. In part this was a decision based on the local authority suggesting the two next nearest schools were currently at capacity and Helena would be required to travel too far to the next school with available places. Personal tutoring was considered a possibility and two tutors worked with Helena briefly; Melanie suggested that they were 'very nice but very expensive' and described how her daughter did not enjoy being taught one-to-one by either of the tutors. During this time Melanie had become a more active participant in her church, (as a child she had attended regularly with her mother but in later life her involvement became irregular). Her children had both begun to attend Sunday morning clubs run by the church.

> It's a very Black church! I took Rob there once and he was like woahhh ... not for me. He's not religious. But I wanted people to meet him there once at least. At the time I started going back I made new friends and there were people I knew from way back. My mother's generation and their children who were grown-up now. And they were supportive. I found out some things about the school that I should have known. That what Jenny had been saying, and what my dad said, was probably true.

At her church Melanie spoke with a number of other parents whose children attended the same primary school as Helena. In many of these conversations racism was cited as an ongoing problem within local schools though it was a problem that was hard to pin down evidentially. One parent described how their quiet, shy son was effectively ignored by another classroom teacher in Helena's school. This parent suggested his son was ignored because he was Black and argued that both the school's head and many of its teachers were racist. Based on her own experience, including the school's response to her criticism, Melanie was less convinced racism was the main or only factor. She noted,

> I still don't feel that's the whole story but it's hard not to think something is happening.

Two strategies for improving her children's educational experience were described to Melanie by other parents in her church. The first was a local Saturday School and the other was home education. The Saturday School was a

108   *Race and ethnicity*

community-run organisation used by many parents at the church which delivered a mix of educational, play and social activities. According to Melanie,

> mostly it was about Black families taking responsibility for their children's lives, building up values and community spirit. Also that the children were great. That they looked out for each other. And that it was a very positive place to be.

Home education was described by the parents of a boy who had experienced aggressive and violent playground bullying which they felt was not dealt with adequately by the school (this was a different school to the one attended by Helena). Melanie described a very emotional conversation with Jenny when she suggested she would not be able to home educate. She was surprised at how scathing Jenny was about the education the school was delivering and how receptive she was to the possibility of home education. At this point she decided not to rule out the possibility of home educating her children despite her instinctive feeling it was the wrong approach. One reason she did not simply dismiss the possibility of home education related to her understanding of her support and social networks. Like many other parents she identified concerns about her daughter not socialising enough with other children and around the practicalities associated with having a child at home all day. She felt her social and family networks would in many ways afford a manageable means to smooth these concerns over. However, she felt the financial consequences of making a decision to home educate could be more significant. In this respect it was less a concern about the immediate loss of a part-time salary, but rather her long-term prospects. Melanie had worked part-time for the same small company for over 10 years and had a good relationship with the directors. When her partner died she had stopped working for them for several years, but they had always promised they would re-employ her in the future; a promise they immediately made good on by offering part-time work based around her childcare responsibilities when she approached them informally. Melanie identified this element of her working life as an important factor in her long-term financial security.

Both Melanie and Jenny visited the Saturday School that had been suggested to them but were unconvinced it was the right place for Helena. In particular Melanie felt uncomfortable with some of the parents and the teachers. Melanie, Helena, Stevie and Jenny visited the Saturday School together and she identified a slightly uncomfortable atmosphere around Jenny's whiteness in the school,

> It was too Black. It felt a bit like a political organisation. In quite a good way but just a bit too 'We are the Black people standing up for our rights'. I felt sorry for Jenny. They were ok with her but it wasn't quite right.

Despite this experience Melanie identified and visited another Saturday School that matched her expectations more closely. Children of different ages took part in a range of activities for three hours on Saturday afternoons in a generally relaxed atmosphere at a local community centre. The school sessions were followed by most parents and children sharing a communal meal. Melanie described how both her children began to attend this Saturday School. Compared to the cost of personal tutors, it was inexpensive and she enjoyed the company of other parents. Melanie described how the school made a virtue of being shaped by the values and experiences of Black and ethnic minority families.

> It *is* only Black families who go here though. Some African but mostly Caribbean. Some White parents though. Like Rob. I tried to explain to my dad on the phone. I said it is about Black families here and now and how our lives have been different to his and mums. And he got that. He knows that I'm not sending Helena to school in Trinidad and that I'm not going to come and live there. For the same reasons my granddad came to Britain. We find something that works where we are now.

She described putting 'home education' on hold as an idea in part because she identified problems around the consequences of home education and the demands it would place on her; but also because, 'it's not me, I'm not that sort of parent'. Rob explained how he felt the family had grown out of a number of chance moments:

> When Helena started at the Saturday School I was getting closer to Mel again. We've always got on but maybe we kept ourselves at a distance. Both of us. I thought oh that's a bonus. I knew she was worried about the school. So that seemed sensible – do some extra lessons. Sort out the problems. And at the same time I was thinking it might be nice we could have a couple hours together on a weekend. Just talking.

Rob was surprised when he realised the Saturday School was not just about childcare but that most of the parents participated more generally in the running and management of activities and communal meals. He described going with Melanie and her children on a daytrip to the seaside at Littlehampton organised by the school.

> I thought about whether I should be there and it was odd. I think maybe there were a couple of other white parents who were in relationships with a Black guy or a Black woman. But that was it. So it was a bit odd. No one said anything and everyone was just having fun. But also it was quite normal. I mean having a barbecue on a cold beach. If it was my family it would be Southend or Margate. But it was the same thing. I felt quite comfortable with what we were all there for.

Describing her thoughts on home education further, Melanie suggested that she had never ruled it out as a possible way forward. After Helena moved

110 *Race and ethnicity*

to secondary school she negotiated with the Local Authority for Stevie to change schools at the beginning of the new school year. At that time he was able to move to a more local school than had previously been available for his sister. During his time at this school Melanie identified problems about the type of education being delivered and also around racist name-calling in the playground. She described how the school dealt quickly and effectively with instances of racism and with bullying more generally; but added,

> I don't think it's a good school. But when they were inspected they got outstanding. I've got a copy of the report. I don't think it's outstanding. Lots of children don't do that well there. What I would say though is that I don't think Stevie's race plays a part. It's a different sort of school to [previous school]. The teachers are very young and very mixed. Racially I mean. Black, White, Chinese. They just seem more a part of the people who live here. They're all women though and some of the other parents they keep going on you need a male teacher. You need a male head teacher. But I don't know. I like the teachers. They just seem to underestimate what the kids could do.

Both children have continued their attendance at Saturday School, but Melanie has never chosen to home educate. Largely this is a decision shaped by Melanie's understandings of the practicalities and priorities in her life. She was constrained financially and the option of giving up work in order to home educate was not realistic. She also identified her personal objections to withdrawing her children from school. For Melanie schooling was a valuable commodity for her family; even ineffective schooling was identified as delivering vital skills, learning and socialisation for her children. Finally, and despite the reassurance of people close to her, Melanie consistently identified her lack of confidence in taking direct responsibility for the children's education. This latter concern was partly framed by her feelings about her own educational achievement; but of greater significance was her weighing up the range of options she could deploy to manage risk in order to ensure the long-term security of her family. Melanie highlighted how risks and missed opportunities that had shaped her life could be exacerbated by choosing home education:

> If it goes wrong that's down to me. I said to Rob I'm not gambling on their lives.

Margaret and Ken Alabi

Margaret and Ken Alabi live in a south-east London suburb with their two children Rita (8) and Charles (13). Ken's parents moved to the UK from Nigeria when he was a baby and he has lived all his life in London. Whilst Margaret's parents also moved to the UK when she was quite young, she and two other siblings remained in Nigeria with her grandparents. She only moved to the UK

Race and ethnicity 111

when she was 13. Both parents described themselves as Christians and regularly attend a Pentecostal church that primarily serves Nigerians.

The Alabis' son Charles attends a voluntary aided Catholic secondary school. However, the family home educated Charles for his last two years of primary education. Rita attends a local primary school. Margaret works as a teaching assistant in a secondary school and Ken is a senior manager in a large civil service department.

Margaret described how both she and her husband had mixed feelings about their children's educational experiences.

> We always push the children to do the very best they can and they recognise that is a good thing. Charles knows, in the future, he wants to make something of himself. And he can do that. But he needs to get the opportunities. He needs to have the chance to take those opportunities. Some of the schools he went to were not so good. Maybe some children had more opportunities and for Charles: No. It wasn't the same.

The Alabis had moved Charles twice whilst attending primary school. They described how they had been initially uncomfortable with the quality of teaching for the reception and early years classes at one school. They arranged for Charles to attend a different primary school but again felt the school was very similar to the first school. When asked to explain in more detail the particular problems they encountered in these schools, both parents described a range of concerns including the relative inexperience and young age of the teachers, their belief that both schools were run in a chaotic fashion with very little discipline and an impression that their son seemed not to progress quickly in key skills such as reading and writing. They finally agreed to another move to a primary school located some distance from where they live when Charles was 7 years old and he remained at that school for the next two years. Ken explained,

> It was a much better school. I read all the government's reports and that was the best school. If you wanted your children to do well that was the school you would send them to. They have better teachers, better parents.

When asked about what this meant in practice, Ken and Margaret described how the teachers appeared to be older and more experienced. They were also initially very impressed with the head teacher.

> Every morning he would stand by the gates. He would say 'good morning' to the children. 'Good morning, Charles. Good morning, Thomas.' He set an example.

And when asked about what was meant by 'better parents', Ken suggested these were 'working parents' and that they were 'well-off, respectable'. Although they

112 Race and ethnicity

were initially comfortable with the school, as Charles progressed both parents felt that he was not doing as well as he was able. In particular they felt that some children were being given a wider range of opportunities than other children. Two moments were described in particular. The first related to a school production at Christmas when all the children in Charles's year were given either a performing role or a backstage role. The Alabis explained how although their son was a talented singer who performed regularly in their church choir, he was given a very minor role in the chorus. They were particularly upset by this and felt the children given more prominent roles delivered noticeably poor performances, including one child whose singing was so quiet no one could hear him. They spoke to Charles's teacher about the performance and were given some assurances that in the future Charles would probably take on bigger roles in school productions. The second moment, and a more important one for the Alabis, emerged around the decision by the school to teach Maths by ability; essentially the year cohort was divided into three groups and Charles was placed in the middle set. Ken described this as 'just plain wrong'.

> My son has a gift for Mathematics. I have worked with him and he is better than me now. It is his gift in life. He's a natural Mathematician. I spoke at first with two of the teachers in the school and they started to explain it was an experiment. That Charles might move up to the next group if he was doing well. It was all about telling me, 'just let us get on with our jobs, we know better than you'. I know my son better.

The Alabis described how they were at the school every day to put pressure on Charles's class teacher to address the problem. They described this as a very 'stressful' time in their lives. They also described how they were asked by the school's head teacher to come into the school for a meeting. Ken was very unhappy with the outcomes of this meeting.

> This was a man I respected. I was always polite when I met him. And he had always been polite with me. That day he made my wife cry. He said we could no longer come on to the school premises if we disagreed with the school. That Charles was going to be moved into a different class because he wanted a fresh start with a new teacher. When I asked him if Charles' Maths group would change he said no. He said wait until half-term and they would assess the groups. He was rude to me. He said this is what is happening, now go.

Following this meeting the Alabis described how they very quickly became involved in a succession of complicated disputes with the school and the local authority. They complained both about the Head's attitude and about their son's experience. They also became aware that another boy in Charles class had been moved from the middle Maths group to the top set. Margaret felt this was clear evidence of discrimination.

Race and ethnicity 113

> [The school] said there would be an assessment of the Maths and then children would be moved. Instead one boy is moved immediately. So the school lied. Why was one boy moved? Immediately I understood we are the wrong sort of people. We have the wrong accent. The wrong skin.

Margaret went on to describe how the boy who was moved up the sets was an Asian boy from a more wealthy background. She discussed how the school attracted largely middle-class parents from its local vicinity. The Alabis lived some distance from the school in a different area. To some extent the Alabis' account of the school demographics was not borne out by its most recent OFSTED report which suggested the school was 'typically diverse' compared to other schools in south-east London both in terms of ethnicity and in terms of social class (based on free school meals' eligibility). That said, local estate agent's descriptions invariably flag up the school as being the best in the area and living within the catchment area is considered a selling point.

Unhappy with both the handling of their son's teaching and also with the response from the school and local authority to their complaints, both parents visited the school again to discuss their options at a meeting convened with the Head and one of the school governors. The Alabis were not told beforehand, but discovered at the meeting that a legal representative of the local authority and another employee of the local authority who took detailed minutes of the meeting were also in attendance. They described how it was much more formal than anticipated and largely did not proceed as they had expected. Early in the meeting Margaret suggested that if their problems were not resolved she would remove Charles from school. Both parents were surprised when the local authority representative began to explain that this was a possible solution and gave them advice on their legal right to home educate. The Head teacher similarly began to explain that this might well be a very effective solution that would allow them a greater say in Charles's education. Ken described how he found this turn of events to be quite shocking.

> I didn't believe their attitude to Charles. They really did not want him in the school. And the lawyer. He was just telling me if you want to take Charles out of school that's fine. When people tell me the British education is the best in the world I just say you need to see what happens here. These people don't care about the children.

The Alabis left this meeting feeling shocked and deeply unhappy with the school and the local authority generally. They withdrew Charles from the school, on what they understood to be a short-term basis, in order to take some time to evaluate their options. Both parents were very taken aback, when almost immediately the local authority wrote to them to suggest the family had agreed to home educate following the meeting at the school. Mr Alabi described how, in this letter, the local authority set out the legal position for home educators, they enclosed a small handbook with useful information and contacts that the

114 Race and ethnicity

Alabis may wish to get in touch with (including local home educator groups), and referred them to a local library in which the authority had funded a home education resource hub. The overall impression given by the Alabis was that they had been pushed, fairly robustly, by the school and local authority into the position of being identified as 'home educators'; and this was because they were labelled as being a difficult family to deal with. Margaret suggested this developed on two inter-related fronts: partly they were the 'wrong type' of parent and partly they challenged what the school had to offer.

> The school didn't want us. They prefer all those rich parents or if you are not rich they want you to keep quiet. If you have money then they will change things for you. And maybe they don't want any Africans. The parents here think the African boys are in gangs. They cause all the trouble. It's not true, it's the parents who don't care whose children are in gangs. The authority think we should all just take what we are given. (Local authority lawyer) said *this is your third school. How many schools do you want?* So it's our fault. We want our son to do well, so we are making a problem.

Discussing the problems the family had encountered, both parents were asked if they felt they handled the school and other officials in an effective fashion. Mr Alabi acknowledged that he always wanted his son in school and therefore the outcome of his engagement had effectively failed. However, he also reiterated Mrs Alabi's suggestion that in part what happened was related to his class status and ethnicity. Mr Alabi felt that certain families' concerns were more likely to be heard and acted upon than others. Wealthier families or families who exhibited higher social status were more likely to be listened to than poorer families. In addition Mr Alabi noted that being Nigerian or African was understood differently.

> [The school] have an idea about Nigerians. We are thieves. Dangerous people. So then, if you are White that's good but only if you are White from here. White people from [well known social housing estate nearby] they don't come to this school. Polish people, Russian people not so good. Asian kids they're ok, the ones round here. Muslims no.

Mr Alabi suggested the school had a range of values associated around class, ethnicity and religion, that were often distinguishable on the basis of geographical proximity to the school. In this respect the types of White and Asian families associated with the school were those who lived very locally and were identified as tending to be middle class and the better cohorts of students. Their parents tended to be identified as having a greater say in what the school should or should not be doing. Mrs Alabi reiterated these distinctions and also made reference back to the school performance. She described how the best parts in the performance, the ones that involved speaking, singing or dancing roles were all assigned to middle-class White and Asian children whilst poorer White, non-British White and Black children were assigned generic chorus roles. (She also recalled how the 'shy' children were responsible for the backstage roles, but even here the two most high-profile roles – lights and sound – were taken by White middle-class children whilst other children were scene-shifters).

The Alabis felt their son was pushed into home education both as a means of avoiding conflict with the family and also because it was an easy option for the school and local authority. The Alabis' description of their relationship with the school suggests some clear ambiguities over whether or not they were overly aggressive on occasion towards the schools. The family showed us some of their correspondence with the school which appears to detail very specific claims of inappropriate and verbally aggressive behaviour by Mrs Alabi towards Charles's classroom teacher. Both Alabis disputed this account. However, within other correspondence there is also very clear evidence that little or no effort is being made to suggest the family keep their son in school.

The family's decision to home educate seems largely driven by the school and local authority management of the situation. Having withdrawn Charles from school, Mrs Alabi undertook responsibility for his day-to-day education for two years until he was of secondary school age. Despite, the family's association with Pentecostalism, Charles was enrolled in a Catholic secondary school and the family are content with his progress there. They explained their choice of school was largely based on their perception of the secondary school as offering a traditional and disciplined environment and one in which a religious element to school life played a significant role.

The family's other child, Margaret, has attended a different primary school and the family have no intention of home educating her. Since Charles began secondary school, Mrs Alabi has worked as a teaching assistant with a view to training as a teacher herself. Neither parent suggested home education would be a choice they would have naturally made and, reflecting on the experience, they both described misgivings about how effective Charles's learning was during this time. They invested some of their resources in home tutoring, but generally this was too expensive an option for the family. Mrs Alabi made some initial links with a group of home educators but felt their perspective on education was very different to her own. In particular she described their commitment to home education rather than schooling as being entirely contrary to her own beliefs, that children should attend school, and to her own situation.

> The mothers in the library group would talk about how children were kicked out of school were not the same. They never said it to my face, but they would talk about bringing the reputation of home education down.

Like the Woods, the Alabis also began to access a Saturday school for both their children, shortly before Charles started at secondary school. They suggested this would have been a useful option for them throughout their children's schooling but that they had not been aware of their existence until late in the day.

116 *Race and ethnicity*

Beck suggests that globalisation

> is a non-linear, dialectic process in which the global and the local do not exist as cultural polarities but as combined and mutually implicating principles. These processes involve not only interconnections across boundaries, but transform the quality of the social and the political inside nation-state societies.
>
> (2002: 17)

Such processes of cosmopolitanisation materialise within the 'ambivalent consequences of globalization in cross-national and multi-local research' (2002: 24). This is clearly seen in the case of the Woods family in which all the different actors understood elements of local and global knowledge to be shaping their identities. This is perhaps most evident in Melanie's management of expectations and aspirations related to her parents' Trinidadian and diasporic lives being framed within a life lived in North London. But, it can also be seen within Rob's encounters with Melanie, her family and her church; despite having lived his whole life in one North London locality, Rob is clearly marked by engagement with a range of discourses that transcend both the local and national. Despite this, the family's decision processes were often very personal and shaped by local and community driven knowledge. Both Melanie and Rob invested heavily within the support networks of friends and family they had grown up with and appeared unlikely to distance themselves from in the future. Beyond looking towards such local networks, they also both appeared to engage in discourses typically shaped by local knowledge. These include traditional accounts of the importance of schooling rather than more novel or radical educational strategies such as homeschooling, or individualised and perhaps more middle-class options, such as private tuition. When the family did engage with a non-traditional educational route, it was Saturday Schools organised by and for a local Black community. Local risks shaped by racism and discrimination were identified, but were managed within community structures that celebrated the global identities of parents, and, recognised them as being reconfigured or reimagined in the present and in local settings. *Roots* were not forgotten, but they were associated with the past and other territories; they were not significant in providing strategies for managing risk in the present. The engagement with and between local communities, churches and Saturday Schools resonated with Castells's account of territorially fixed, urban social movements capable of delivering social change, and which 'mobilize around . . . collective consumption, cultural identity, and political self-management' (1983: 328). Global and cosmopolitan identities in this setting work to change and counter local risks.

For Melanie home education was one alternative option she could use to manage risks that perhaps materialised out of her cosmopolitan life; it was an option she first encountered as a proposed solution to local racism, and it was an option that identified potential strategies to resolve divergent issues in her

Race and ethnicity   117

life. Her decision *not* to home educate (and it is worth remembering in a book about decisions to home educate that Melanie's choice is a more common outcome than the examples of other parents in this research), reflected both the practicalities of being poorer rather than wealthier, the availability of other strategies and a world-view in which schooling remained preferable. For the Alabis, a somewhat different pattern emerged, not least because they felt they were pushed towards a decision to home educate rather than it being a choice they would automatically make. In this process it is hard not to think the school was identifying *risks*, framed by cosmopolitan understandings of class and race in South London schools. To manage these risks schools and local authorities potentially distribute opportunity to certain groups but not others; and in doing so, appease and embrace some parents and some families whilst actively excluding others. Such a strategy might well be an effective structural means of managing the risks schools identify such as failing in league tables or poor OFSTED reports; and, in the Alabis' situation, the risk of engaging in time-consuming management of dissatisfied parents.

Neither the Alabis nor the Woods appeared well-served by their local schools, despite all the different schools they had accessed being categorised as 'good' or 'outstanding' by OFSTED. This was reflected throughout the accounts of other Black and minority ethnic parents, including Gypsy and Traveller and Muslim families. It was also evident in the accounts given by other categories of parents such as those whose children had special educational needs. Often what emerges is a sense that schools fail certain categories of people, and this is reinforced because of increasing shifts towards the commodification of schools. The pressure of managing schools within a free-market does not lend itself to making adaptations to difference, one consequence being the emergence of different educational economies. Home education is one such emergent market and others include Saturday Schools and the increasing use of private tuition. In accessing different economies there is some evidence to suggest parents gravitate towards other parents like themselves. This reflects the localised nature of such solutions. The Saturday Schools that appeal to Black parents linked by mutual cultural experiences, geographies and shared aspirations are mirrored in the home education support groups that Margaret Alabi found uncomfortable to attend because she was different to these parents. Ethnicity as well as class, religion and personal experience shape the new boundaries within which education and home education are being delivered.

9   Conclusions

Home education, risk and belonging

In this book, we have argued that concerns about home education have been repeatedly framed in terms of risk to children. Unsurprisingly, our research argues that many home educators object to such accounts. Rather, we find that the processes which families go through in order to home educate their children, for the most part can be understood as narratives in which parents are actively seeking to achieve the best outcomes for their children. Early in this book we argued that 'heterogeneity rules' both in terms of diversity in class, ethnicity and the relative affluence of different families, but also in terms of the reasons underpinning the decisions to home educate; and, it is also the case in terms of the type of home education different home educators deliver. Despite these differences what remains clear in our research was that families reflected on their decisions to home educate; they often worried about whether they were doing the right thing and actively sought to achieve the best outcomes for their children. In this respect of course they had much in common with many other families whose children attend school, who also reflect and worry about how best to educate their children to ensure their future happiness and security.

The clearest distinction to be drawn between different types of home educators in our research was between families who appeared to have greater control over the choices they made for their children and families who felt they had less control. The former tended to include middle-class and more affluent families, who often made 'lifestyle' choices from a range of options rather than being forced into a narrow set of choices. The latter tended to be families for whom schooling became almost impossible and the decision to home educate was one of fewer options left available.

In the UK accounts of risk have been associated with how families have been *perceived* as home educators and have focused around two specific concerns: risks associated with the well-being of children, (as identified in the Badman Review), and risks related to potential Islamic radicalisation and fostering of anti-British values, (as identified by OFSTED). These risks and the perception of them are neither real nor imaginary in a quantifiable sense, rather they are potential outcomes. The nature of risk, that it will occur in the future but is assessed and managed in the present (Douglas and Wildavsky, 1982), makes many home educators very uncomfortable. The assessment of their personal,

Conclusions 119

family decision-making seemingly called into question for potential future crimes. They perceive more than a whiff of a dystopian clamp-down; precrime as an ideological authoritarian tool to restrict their personal rights (Dick, 1956/2002). Such objections are seemingly both rational yet unrealistic. Their rationality reflects perceptions that the state does not always act in the interest of its citizens; this is reflected in the United States experience of home education of radicals on the left and right identifying the personal importance in distancing their children and family from state education (Stevens, 2001). They are also unrealistic in large part because all states do interfere in the lives of citizens: citizenship is not a personal relationship but membership of a wider body of regulation and social agreement. Home educators could also be accused of deliberately embracing a degree of tunnel-vision regarding their wider social membership. Just as states identify and act on potential risks; so too do many home educators whose decisions are predicated on their perception and management of risk. Home educators understand the pitfalls of schooling and actively manage their children's education just like many other families.

Middle-class home educators recognise failing schools and they make assessments about what works best for their children. They identify the potential risks of the future by managing and deploying their resources in order to maintain their children's well-being, safety and success. This is not a new and surprising development; there have always been anomalies in educational provision and parents have always worked to make the best of opportunities such anomalies offered their children. In the past middle-class families have often successfully developed strategies to privilege their children's outcomes despite attempts at introducing more socially equitable structures for schooling (Reay, 2017). Potentially the increasing push towards greater marketisation of schools creates wider and more glaring anomalies; and in our research, it often appeared that many middle-class home educators were identifying new positions within a changing educational field. The narrative in which parents are expected to exercise 'choice' is one in which there are greater options and greater change. Schools are more clearly delineated by geographical location, by league tables and by funding arrangements. In our research, it often felt as though those parents who most closely identified these changing patterns in schooling and then made the decision to home educate were the ones who were 'ahead of the game'. Such parents demonstrated a confidence borne out of their instinctive *sense* of the scale of current changes within education to make the boldest decisions. If they felt 'out of time' in the present, this might be because they anticipated how best to deploy their present resources to position themselves for the future.

We argue that for these families, choosing to home educate was simply the deployment of their resources in a similar fashion to other middle-class parents; they used the economic, social and cultural capital at their disposal in order to guarantee the best future and security for their children. For such parents the wise investment of such capitals within their children's education can reap the significant reward of greater economic, social and cultural capital in the future.

120   *Conclusions*

The principles of such strategies are well understood; but unlike other parents, home educators potentially identify the changing landscape of the educational field differently. They appear to be playing by the wrong rules because they are simply ahead of the game, what Bourdieu might describe as 'the *hysteresis effect*' (1977: 78). The association of risk and home education is one that compounds temporal dislocations because the identification and management of risk are predicated on responding to an unknown future. Such futures, as Beck (1992, 2006) suggests, have changed exponentially because the management of risks, no longer bounded by national borders or controls, has changed the minutiae of individual's lives. This is a high stakes game: families are required to put their capitals at risk, to back their own strategies and reap the consequences. In the past their children's futures were managed more centrally, by risk determined largely by educational policies that easily replicated traditional class structures. Now, their sense of the risks and the choices available has a much greater impact on their personal lives. The potential is that home educators, still the exception rather than the rule, in confronting risk and the future more directly, 'incur negative sanctions' because 'the environment with which they are confronted is too distant from that which they are objectively fitted' (Bourdieu, 1977: 78). They identify 'different definitions of the impossible, the possible, and the probable' as 'natural or reasonable practices or aspirations' (Bourdieu, 1977: 78), but which more commonly are associated with difficult, problematic, anti-social and risky behaviour.

One signal that home educators are ahead of the game, that they are exhibiting characteristics that are becoming more acceptable as they evidence their success and that the deployment of capital is not a risky gamble but a risk-reducing strategy, is perhaps most evident in the emergent narratives about risk and certain types of home educators. In these narratives it often appears it is the *type* of home educator who is a risk rather than the *practice* of home education itself. Media accounts of home educators tend to present one of two accounts. In the first a middle-class family's exciting and challenging leap into a world of adventure and newfound freedoms is described. These stories often appear within the family, leisure or travel supplements of newspapers. The choices that are shown often appear closer to a family embarking on an extended holiday but in the context of the difficulties of balancing educational and family pressures. The alternative narrative, and the narrative that is often found to be making front page headlines, is the depressing account of poor, inadequate families for whom home education represents their falling off social services' radar. These families are lost from the system and the support they need; their children starve to death or suffer harrowing stories of neglect. Against this backdrop other official narratives emerge in which minority groups, including Gypsy and Muslim families, are identified as problematic home educators. In all these cases home education is used as an alternative means to promulgate existing biases and racisms. Partly this relates to specific racisms faced by Gypsies and Muslims in schools, but it also relates to a wider construction of British identity and British values. If middle-class home educators are ahead of the game now, in the future

Conclusions 121

it seems a safe assumption that a realignment of understanding of home education will accommodate their behaviours. There is evidence that this is already happening in the UK. The main recommendations of the Badman Review was for a number of legislative changes which, in comparison to the protections afforded children's rights more generally in the UK, were fairly modest. Badman suggested the introduction of registration schemes for home-educated children and for local authorities to have some limited access to visit such children. These changes were not implemented at the time, despite the strong support of the then Education Minister, largely because the timing in the run-up to a general election was politically unhelpful. But since then neither the Coalition government nor the current Conservative government have made any attempt to take this forward. The most recent pressure from OFSTED for similar changes does so in its very narrow discourse around Muslim families and threats to British values. There appears to be little political will to introduce any legislation that would impact on home education or home educators.

In the context of managing risk, the very local risks that emerge in discourses around home education are not the risks that are informing policy making. On the one hand, this includes concerns about child neglect or abuse; on the other it also includes the issues parents identify about their experience of schools. Parents often described very specific local concerns that contributed to their decision to home educate, including the lack of effective provision for children with special educational needs, bullying and racism. In addition a number of parents suggested they felt pressured into home educating by schools and local authorities because of disputes with the school. In these instances decisions to home educate are signals of the risk that schools are failing to address the needs of all pupils. However, in the concentration on risks associated with particular types of home educators rather than home education practice, it is the wider risks of citizenship and nation building that seem to be prioritised not the risks of failing schools or failing parents. The identities of those already on the inside are readily protected or at the very least tolerated whilst those on the outside are repelled. For many middle-class home educators this is an effective field in which they can operate – their more cosmopolitan identities aligning with a neo-liberal discourse that promotes exercising choice in the education markets. Other less cosmopolitan, already marginal groups are less favourably perceived, not least because of their evidential lack of success. They are not making effective choices between a competitive range of enticing educational offers; they simply have to take what's on offer. Whilst these families are also managing their lives at a local level, it is with far less certainty about outcomes.

One argument regularly promoted by home educators, particularly in the United States, is that it is a traditional practice and that schooling is both a new and a retrograde step (Gaither, 2008). However, this argument fails to acknowledge historical and social change (Katz, 1987) in any meaningful way and confuses the choices made by homeschoolers with the objective realities of the past and the subjective lived experience of families in the present. The nostalgia that attaches itself to these accounts does a disservice to other more

122 Conclusions

radical interpretations of engaging in highly localised, family-centric educational practice. These might include Beck's (1992) 'negotiated family' in which more democratic, individualised identities emerge within family structures as the state's influence declines. If the normative, global shift is moving towards homogenised schooling and the privileging of children's rights, this raises questions about the value of individualised educational practice. It could be that 'negotiated families' position themselves differently; potentially they could more astutely deploy their resources to manage their position within new, global and homogenous identities. If the whole world is learning the same way, then home educators potentially have the creativity and confidence to challenge the global masses and create new elites.

The evidence from research around homeschooling in the United States tends not to support such a vision of the future. Apple (2005) suggests a new conservative politics dominated by white, middle- and working-class families with strong evangelical religious beliefs and traditional attitudes towards gender and sexuality that parallels a wide swathe of homeschoolers' belief and practice. The 'home' becomes an inward-looking re-imagination of how family life can materialise within such traditionally held world views. It mirrors the sentiments of Donald Trump's insular economic and foreign policies marking a retreat from an engagement with the outside world. Whilst homeschoolers seemingly do identify transnational risk in very material ways, they also identify intensely local solutions characterised by a return to small-scale, homely safety of the family. Whilst Apple (2005) has argued that this homely identity is also characterised by being well-organised and strategic, the ambitions of such homeschoolers seem limited and in retreat from a wider engagement with communities beyond their own very narrow experience. Whilst the 'business' of homeschooling is flourishing in the United States, it could be tied to a declining accumulation of useful capitals within families. Such strategies resonate with domestic policies informed by building walls, closing borders and pulling the shutters down.

The families in our research appeared to demonstrate a wider range of possibilities about home education than that evidenced in research from the United States. Notwithstanding the evidence that different groups increasingly do choose to homeschool in the United States (Murphy, 2012), there is a predominance of a single type of home educator: white, conservative and evangelical. This is not replicated in the UK. Our own research identified much greater diversity not just in terms of what sort of people home educate but also in terms of their personal beliefs.

However, the families in our research also associated home education with intimacy and close family relationships. For many home educators there was also a relationship between home and community identities; this crossed religious, ethnic and to a lesser extent class lines. The importance of home and community was highly significant in the lives of Muslim and Plymouth Brethren families and also in those of Gypsy families. It also seemed more significant in terms of families who had children with disabilities or who identified as having special educational needs. However, for the more affluent families the home remained important but situated in wider social contexts. Their reliance on strong social bonds appeared more outward-looking and more likely to go beyond the immediate confines of family and community. Possibly this suggests that in many ways the strategic advantages of risk management in the United Kingdom are emerging in a more cosmopolitan fashion than is reported in the United States.

Throughout our research many different families identified the importance of local self-help groups and self-organised collectives. For families who felt schools had failed their children and who did not rely heavily on community support, the importance of informally organised groups was a common part of their daily routines. Some of these groups were specifically focused around local groups of home educators. Others such as Saturday Schools functioned in similar ways but in response to the needs of wider groups of families dissatisfied with local schools, but were also often used by home educators. For Black families the importance of Saturday Schools was often linked not just to the educational and social aspects of joining together with like-minded families, but also a sense in which their identities, shaped by global diaspora and local experience were shared. Like more affluent families, they often readily acknowledged the broader global experience. Often the risks they appeared to manage were specifically local, such as their experiences of racism in schools, but these were framed within an understanding that their lives were directly linked to other places and that their children's experiences would draw upon a different set of experiences to those of their parents or their grandparents.

Early in this book we noted that the question 'is home education a good thing?' is often at the heart of accounts of home education. This seems the wrong question to ask. Different home educators home educate differently. Some do it well and some do it less well; just as some children who attend school receive a good education and some do not. There is a strong indication that inequalities in education generally are also prevalent in home education. The identification of the risks associated with home educators reflects wider biases about class and ethnicity. The successful management of risk by home educators reflects very traditional patterns in which those families with access to economic, social and cultural capital are best placed to protect their own interests.

References

Apple, M. W. (2000) The cultural politics of home schooling. *Peabody Journal of Education*, *75*, 1–2: 256–271.

Apple, M. W. (2005) Education, markets and an audit culture. *Critical Quarterly*, *47*, 1–2: 11–29.

Apple, M. W. (2006a) *Educating the "right" way: Markets, standards, God, and inequality*. London: Taylor and Francis.

Apple, M. W. (2006b) The complexities of black home schooling. *Teachers College Record*. Accessed December 12, 2012.

Apple, M. W. (2007) Curriculum planning: Content, form and the politics of accountability. In Connelly, F., Phillon, J. and Fang He, M. (eds) *The SAGE handbook of curriculum and instruction*. London: Sage.

Apple, M. W. (2015) Education as God wants it: Gender, labour and home schooling. In *International perspectives on home education* (pp. 286–299). Basingstoke: Palgrave Macmillan.

Arai, A. (2000) Reasons for home schooling in Canada. *Canadian Journal of Education*, *25*: 204–217.

Arora, T. C. (2003) School-aged children who are educated at home by their parents: Is there a role for educational psychologists? *Educational Psychology in Practice*, *19*, 2: 103–112.

Arora, T. C. (2006) Elective home education and special educational needs. *Journal of Research in Special Education*, *26*, 1: 55–66.

Badman Review (2009) *Report to the secretary of state on elective home education*. London: HMSO.

Basham, P., Merrifield, J. and Hepburn, C. R. (2007) *Home schooling: From the extreme to the mainstream*. Vancouver: Fraser Institute.

Baker, D. and LeTendre, G. K. (2005) *National differences, global similarities: World culture and the future of schooling*. Stanford, CA: Stanford University Press.

Bauman, Z. (1997) The making and unmaking of strangers. In Werbner, P. and Modood, T. (eds) *Debating cultural hybridity*. London: Zed Books.

Bauman, Z. (2000) *Liquid modernity*. Cambridge: Polity.

Beck, U. (1992) *Risk society: Towards a new modernity*. London: Sage.

Beck, U. (2002) The cosmopolitan society and its enemies. *Theory, Culture & Society*, *19*, 1–2: 17–44.

Beck, U. (2006) *The cosmopolitan vision*. Cambridge: Polity.

Beck, U., Bonss, W. and Lau, C. (2003) The theory of reflexive modernization: Problematic, hypotheses and research programme. *Theory, Culture & Society*, *20*, 2: 1–33.

Belfield, C. (2004) Home-schoolers: How well do they perform on the SAT for college admissions? In Cooper, B. (ed) *Home schooling in full view* (pp. 167–178). Greenwich, CT: IAP.

Beveridge, W. H. (1943) *Social insurance and allied services*. London: HMSO.

Bhatia, S. and Ram, A. (2009) Theorizing identity in transnational and diaspora cultures: A critical approach to acculturation. *International Journal of Intercultural Relations, 33*, 2: 140–149.

Bhopal, K. (2004) Gypsy Travellers and education: Changing needs and changing perceptions. *British Journal of Educational Studies, 52*, 1: 47–64.

Bhopal, K. and Myers, M. (2008) *Insiders, outsiders and others: Gypsies and identity.* Hertfordshire: University of Hertfordshire Press.

Bhopal, K. and Myers, M. (2016) Marginal groups in marginal times: Gypsy and Traveller parents and home education in England, UK. *British Journal of Educational Research, 41*, 1: 5–20.

Bourdieu, P. (1977) *Outline of a theory of practice.* Cambridge: Cambridge University Press.

Bourdieu, P. and Passeron, J. (1977) *Reproduction in education, society and culture.* London: Sage.

Casa-Nova, M. J. (2007) Gypsies, ethnicity and the labour market: An introduction. *Romani Studies, 5*, 1: 103–123.

Castells, M. (1983) *The city and the grassroots: A cross-cultural theory of urban social movements.* London: Edward Arnold Ltd.

Cibulka, J. (1991) State regulation of home schooling: A policy analysis. In Van Galen, J. and Pittman, M. (eds) *Home schooling: Political, historical and pedagogical perspectives* (pp. 102–121). Norwood, NJ: Ablex.

Cohen, S. (1972) *Folk devils and moral panics: The creation of the mods and rockers.* London: Routledge.

Collom, E. (2005) The ins and outs of home schooling. *Education and Urban Society, 37*, 3: 307–335.

Conroy, J. C. (2010) The state, parenting, and the populist energies of anxiety. *Educational Theory, 60*, 3: 325–340.

Cooper, B. S. and Sureau, J. (2007) The politics of homeschooling: New developments, new challenges. *Educational Policy, 21*, 1: 110–131.

D'Arcy, K. (2014) *Travellers and home education.* London: IOE, Trentham.

D'Arcy, K. (2017) Using counter-stories to challenge stock stories about Traveller families. *Race, Ethnicity and Education, 20*, 5: 636–649.

Dahlquist, K., York-Barr, J. and Hendel, D. D. (2006) The Choice to Homeschool: Home Educator Perspectives and School District Options. *Journal of School Leadership, 16*, 4: 354–385.

Department for Education (DfE) (2013a) *Elective home education: Guidelines for local authorities.* London: Department for Education.

Department for Education (DfE) (2013b) *National curriculum in England: Citizenship programmes of study for key stages 3 and 4.* London: Department for Environment. www.gov.uk/government/publications/national-curriculum-in-england-citizenship-programmes-of-study/national-curriculum-in-england-citizenship-programmes-of-study-for-key-stages-3-and-4 accessed 14 November 2017.

Department for Education (DfE) (2014) *The Equality Act 2010 and schools: Departmental advice for school leaders, school staff, governing bodies and local authorities.* London: Department for Education.

Derrington, C. (2007) Fight, flight and playing white: An examination of coping strategies adopted by Gypsy Traveller adolescents in English secondary schools. *International Journal of Educational Research, 46*, 6: 357–367.

Derrington, C. and Kendall, S. (2008) Challenges and barriers to secondary education: The experiences of young Gypsy Traveller students in English secondary schools. *Social Policy and Society, 7*, 1: 119–128.

Dick, P. K. (1956/2002). *The Minority Report* (the collected shorts stories of Philip K. Dick). London: Gollancz.

126 References

Donnelly, M. (2012) Homeschooling. In Glenn, C. and De Groof, J. (eds) *Balancing freedom autonomy and accountability in education* (pp. 12–23). Netherlands: Wolf Legal Publishers.

Douglas, M. and Wildavsky, A. (1982) *Risk and culture: An essay on the selection of technical and environmental dangers*. Berkeley, CA: University of California Press.

Duvall, S. (2005) The effectiveness of home schooling students with special needs. In Cooper, B. (ed) *Home schooling in full view: A reader* (pp. 1515–166). Greenwich, CT: Information Age Publishing.

Education Act (1996) London: HMSO.

Education Otherwise (2017) *The current legal status of HE*. https://educationotherwise.org/index.php/current-legal-status accessed 28 November 2017.

Equality Act (2010) London: HMSO. www.legislation.gov.uk/ukpga/2010/15/pdfs/ukpga_20100015_en.pdf accessed 8 September 2017.

Esping-Andersen, G. (2013) *The three worlds of welfare capitalism*. Sussex: John Wiley and Sons.

Evans, Dennis L. (2003). Home is no place for school. *USA Today*, www.usatoday.com/news/opinion/editorials/2003-09-02-opposee_x.htm.

Fields-Smith, C. (2016) Homeschooling among ethnic-minority populations. In Gaither, M. (ed) *The Wiley handbook of home education* (pp. 207–221). Sussex: John Wiley and Sons.

Fields-Smith, C. and Williams, M. (2009) Motivations, sacrifices, and challenges: Black parents' decisions to home school. *The Urban Review*, *41*, 4: 369–389.

Fortune-Wood, M. (2005) *The face of home based education 1: Who, why and how*. Nottingham: Educational Heretics Press.

Foster, D. (2015) *Home education SN/SP/5108*. London: House of Commons Library.

Gabb, S. (2004) *Home schooling: A British perspective*. www.seangabb.co.uk/academic/home schooling.htm

Gaither, M. (2008) Homeschool. In Gaither, M. (ed) *An American history*. London: Palgrave Macmillan.

Giddens, A. (1991) *Modernity and self-identity: Self and society in the late modern age*. Stanford, CA: Stanford University Press.

Gilroy, P. (2002) *There ain't no Black in the union Jack*. London: Taylor and Francis.

Grady, S. (2017) *A fresh look at homeschooling. NCES Blog*. National Centre for Education Statistics. https://ies.ed.gov/blogs/nces/post/a-fresh-look-at-homeschooling-in-the-u-s accessed 30 November 2017.

Hall, S. (2003) Cultural identity and diaspora. In Braziel, J. and Mannur, A. (eds) *Theorizing diaspora*. Oxford: Blackwell Publishing Ltd.

Hardenbergh, N. (2015) Validity of high stakes standardized test requirements for homeschoolers: A psychometric analysis. In Rothermel, P. (ed) *International perspectives on home education* (pp. 111–135). Basingstoke: Palgrave Macmillan.

Hartley, J. (2004). Case study research. In Cassell, C. and Symon, G. (eds) *Essential guide to qualitative methods in organizational research* (pp.323–333). London: Sage.

Hepburn, C. and Van Belle, R. (2003) *The Canadian education freedom index*. Vancouver: The Fraser Institute.

Hill, P. T. (2000) Home schooling and the future of public education. *Peabody Journal of Education*, *75*, 1–2: 20–31.

Holt, J. (1969) *The underachieving school*. New York, NY: Pitman.

Holt, J. (1982) *Teach your own*. New York: Delta Trade Paperbacks.

Hopwood, V., O'Neill, L., Castro, G. and Hodgson, B. (2007) *The prevalence of home education in England: A feasibility study*. Nottingham: DfES.

Houston, R. (1999) *The economic determinants of home education*. Doctoral dissertation, University of Kentucky.

References 127

Huerta, L. (2000) Losing public accountability: A home schooling charter. In Fuller, B. (ed) *Inside charter schools: The paradox of radical decentralization* (pp. 177–202). Cambridge, MA: Harvard University Press.

Isenberg, E. J. (2007) What have we learned about homeschooling? *Peabody Journal of Education, 82,* 2–3: 387–409.

Isenberg, E. J. (2016) Using survey data sets to study homeschooling. In Gaither, M. (ed) *The Wiley handbook of home education* (p. 32). Sussex: John Wiley and Sons.

Ivatts, A. (2006) *The situation regarding the current policy, provision and practice in elective home education (EHE) for Gypsy/Roma and Traveller children.* London: Department for Education and Skills.

Jeffreys, B. (2015) Rising numbers of pupils home educated. *BBC Family and Education.* 21 December 2015. www.bbc.co.uk/news/education-35133119 accessed 16 December 2017.

Jones-Sanpei, Hinckley, A. (2008) Practical school choice in the United States: A proposed taxonomy and estimates of use. *Journal of School Choice, 2,* 3: 318–337.

Katz, M. B. (1987) *Reconstructing American education.* Boston, MA: Harvard University Press.

Knowles, J., Marlow, S. and Muchmore, J. (1992) From pedagogy to ideology: Origins and phases of home education in the United States. *American Journal of Education, 100:* 195–235.

Koons, C. (2010) Home education in the European Union and the need for unified European policy. *Indiana International and Comparative Law Review, 20:* 145.

Kostelecká, Y. (2010) Home education in the post-communist countries: Case study of the Czech Republic. *International Electronic Journal of Elementary Education 3,* 1: https://files.eric.ed.gov/fulltext/EJ1052439.pdf

Kraftl, P. (2013) Towards geographies of "alternative" education: A case study of UK home schooling families. *Transactions of the Institute of British Geographers, 38,* 3: 436–450.

Kunzman, R. (2009) *Home schooling in Indiana: A closer look.* Bloomington, IN: Indiana University, Centre for Evaluation and Education Policy.

Levinson, M. P. (2015) "What's the plan?" "What plan?" Changing aspirations among Gypsy youngsters, and implications for future cultural identities and group membership. *British Journal of Sociology of Education, 36,* 8: 1149–1169.

Levinson, M. P. and Sparkes, A. C. (2004) Gypsy identity and orientations to space. *Journal of Contemporary Ethnography, 33,* 6: 704–734.

Lines, P. (1991) Home instruction: The size and growth of the movement. In Van Galen, J. and Pitmman, M. (eds) *Homeschooling: Political, historical and pedagogical perspectives* (pp. 84–101). San Francisco, CA: Josey Bass.

Lines, P. (2000) When home schoolers go to school: A partnership between families and schools. *Peabody Journal of Education, 75:* 159–186.

Lips, D. and Feinberg, E. (2008) *Homeschooling: A growing option in American education.* Washington, DC: Heritage Foundation.

Lubeke, R. (1999) *Home schooling in Wisconsin: A review of current issues and trends.* Milwaukee, WI: Wisconsin Policy Research Institute.

Lubienski, C. (2000) Whither the common good? A critique of home schooling. *Peabody Journal of Education, 75,* 1–2: 207–232.

Lyman, L. (2000) *The home schooling revolution.* Manchester: Bench Print International.

Mansell, W. and Edwards, P. (2016) DIY schooling on the rise as more parents opt for home education. *The Guardian.* 20 April 2016. London: Guardian Media Group.

Marshall, T. H. 1950 (1964) *Citizenship and social class and other essays.* Cambridge: University of Cambridge Press. [This work was later published in 1964 as *Class, Citizenship and Social development,* 1964 London: Heinemann].

Marshall, T. H. (1990) *Citizenship and social class,* reprinted in Marshall and Bottomore (1992). London: Pluto Press.

128   References

Marshall, T. H. and Bottomore, T. B. (1992) *Citizenship and social class* (Vol. 2). London: Pluto Press.

Martin-Chang, S., Gould, O. N. and Meuse, R. E. (2011) The impact of schooling on academic achievement: Evidence from homeschooled and traditionally schooled students. *Canadian Journal of Behavioural Science/Revue canadienne des sciences du comportement, 43*, 3: 195.

Martin-Chang, S. and Levesque, K. (2016) Academic achievement. In Gaither, M. (ed) *The Wiley handbook of home education* (pp. 121–134). Sussex: John Wiley and Sons.

Mayberry, M., Knowles, G., Ray, B. and Marlow, S. (1995) *Home schooling: Parents as educators.* Thousand Oaks, CA: Corwin.

Mazama, A. and Musumunu, G. (2014) *African Americans and homeschooling: Motivations, opportunities and challenges.* London and New York: Routledge.

Mckeon, C. (2007) *A mixed methods analysis of home schooling styles, instructional practices and reading methodologies.* Doctoral dissertation, Capella University, Minneapolis.

Medlin, R. (2000) Home schooling and the question of socialisation. *Peabody Journal of Education, 75*: 107–123.

Meyer, H. D. (2001) Civil society and education: The return of an idea. In Boyd, W. (ed) *Education between states, markets and civil society: Comparative perspectives* (pp. 13–34). New York, NY: Routledge.

Miron, G., Horvitz, B., Gulosino, C., Huerta, L., Rice, J. K., Shafer, S. R. and Cuban, L. (2013) *Virtual schools in the US 2013: Politics, performance, policy, and research evidence.* National Education Policy Center: Colorado

Moore, R. and Moore, D. (1994) *The successful home school family handbook: A creative and stress free approach to home schooling.* Camas, WA: Institute of Education Sciences.

Murphy, J. (2012) *Homeschooling in America: Capturing and assessing the movement.* Thousand Oaks, CA: Corwin Press.

Musumunu, G. and Mazama, A. (2015) The search for school safety and the African American homeschooling experience. *Journal of Contemporary Issues in Education, 9*, 2.

Myers, M. (2018) Gypsy students in the UK: The impact of mobility on education. *Race, Ethnicity and Education, 21*, 3: 353–369. https://doi.org/10.1080/13613324.2017.1395323

Myers, M. and Bhopal, K. (2009) Gypsy, Roma and Traveller children in schools: Understandings of community and safety. *British Journal of Educational Studies, 57*, 4: 18–26.

Myers, M. and Bhopal, K. (2018) Muslims, home education and risk in British society. Special Issue: Educating British Mulsims: Identity, religion and politics in a neo-liberal era. *British Journal of Sociology of Education, 39*, 2: 212–226

Myers, M., McGhee, D. and Bhopal, K. (2010) At the crossroads – Gypsy, Roma and Traveller parents perceptions of education, protection and social change – observations from a pilot study. *Race, Ethnicity and Education, 13*, 4: 533–548.

National Centre for Education Statistics (NCES) (2016) *Homeschooling in the United States: 2012* (NCES 2016–096). Washington, DC: National Centre for Education Statistics, Institute of Education Science, US Department of Education.

Neuman, W. (1997) *Social research methods: Qualitative and quantitative approaches.* Boston: Allyn and Bacon.

Neuman, A. and Aviram, A. (2003) Homeschooling as a fundamental change in lifestyle. *Evaluation & Research in Education, 17*, 2–3: 132–143.

Neuman, A. and Guterman, O. (2016) Academic achievements and homeschooling – it all depends on the goals. *Studies in Educational Evaluation, 51*, 1–6.

NCLB (*No Child Left Behind*) (2001) Washington, DC: US Act of Congress.

OFSTED (2010) *Local authorities and home education.* London: OFSTED.

References 129

OFSTED (2015a) *Advice note from Sir Michael Wilshaw, her Majesty's Chief Inspector, on the latest position with schools in Birmingham and Tower Hamlets.* London: OFSTED.

OFSTED (2015b) *Advice letter from Sir Michael Wilshaw, her Majesty's Chief Inspector, on unregistered schools.* 10 November 2015. London: OFSTED.

OFSTED (2015c) *Advice letter from Sir Michael Wilshaw, her Majesty's Chief Inspector, on unregistered schools.* 11 December 2015. London: OFSTED.

OFSTED (2016) *Advice letter from Sir Michael Wilshaw, her Majesty's Chief Inspector in respect of suspected illegal schools.* London: OFSTED.

Pattison, H. (2015) How to desire differently: Home education as a heterotopia. *Journal of Philosophy of Education, 49,* 4: 619–637.

Petrie, A. J. (1995) Home education and the law within Europe. *International Review of Education, 41,* 3–4: 285–296.

Petrie, A. J. (2001) Home education in Europe and the implementation of changes to the law. *International Review of Education, 47,* 5: 477–500.

Planty, M., Hussar, W. and Snyder, T. (2009) *The condition of education report.* Washington, DC: NCES.

Putnam, R. D. (2000) *Bowling alone: The collapse and revival of American community.* New York, NY: Simon & Schuster.

Putnam, R. D., Feldstein, L. and Cohen, D. J. (2004) *Better together: Restoring the American community.* New York, NY: Simon and Schuster.

Ray, B. (1997) *Strengths of their own: Home schoolers across America.* Salem, OR: National Home Education Research Institute.

Ray, B. (2005) A home school research story. In Cooper, B. (ed) *Home schooling in full view* (pp. 1–19). Greenwich, CT: Information Age.

Ray, B. D. (2013) Homeschooling associated with beneficial learner and societal outcomes but educators do not promote it. *Peabody Journal of Education, 88,* 3: 324–341.

Ray, B. D. and Eagleson, B. (2008) State regulation of homeschooling and homeschooler's Sat scores. *Academic Leadership Live, the Online Journal, 6*: 3.

Reay, D. (2017) *Miseducation: Inequality, education and the working class.* Bristol: Policy Press.

Redford, J., Battle, D. and Bielick, S. (2016) *Homeschooling in the United States: 2012* (NCES 2016–096). Washington, DC: National Center for Education Statistics, Institute of Education Sciences, U.S. Department of Education.

Reich, R. (2005) Why home schooling should be regulated. In Cooper, B. (ed) *Home schooling in full view* (pp. 109–120). Greenwich, CT: Information Age.

Ricoeur, P. (1980) Narrative time. *Critical Inquiry, 7,* 1: 169–190.

Rothermel, P. (2011) Setting the record straight: Interviews with a hundred British home educating Families. *Journal of Unschooling and Alternative Learning, 5*: 10.

Rothermel, P. (2015) *International perspectives on home education: Do we still need schools?* Basingstoke: Palgrave Macmillan.

Rousseau, J-J. (1959) *Les Rêveries du Promeneur Solitaire,* "Cinquième Promenade". In Chez, J. (ed) *Oeuvres Complètes.* Paris: Gallimard.

Rudner, L. M. (1999) Scholastic achievement and demographic characteristics of home school students in 1998. *Education Policy Analysis Archives, 7,* 8: n8.

Schemmer, B. A. S. (1985) *Case studies of four families engaged in home education.* EdD dissertation, Ball State University.

Scott, A. (2000) Risk society or angst society? Two views of risk, consciousness and community. In Beck, U., Adam, B. and Lon, J. (eds) *The risk society and beyond: Critical issues for social theory* (pp. 33–46). London: Sage.

130   *References*

Smith, D. and Greenfields, M. (2012) Housed Gypsies and Travellers in the UK: Work, exclusion and adaptation. *Race & Class*, *53*, 3: 48–64.

Smith, E. and Nelson, J. (2015) Using the opinions and lifestyle survey to examine the prevalence and characteristics of families who home educate in the UK. *Educational Studies*, *41*, 3: 312–333.

Somerville, S. (2005) Legal rights for home school families. In Cooper, B. (Ed) *Home schooling in full view* (pp. 135–149). Greenwich, CT: Information Age.

Stevens, M. (2001) *Kingdom of children: Culture and controversy in the homeschooling movement.* Princeton, NJ: Princeton University Press.

Stevens, M. L. (2002) The organizational vitality of conservative protestantism. In *Social structure and organizations revisited* (pp. 337–360). Bingley: Emerald Group Publishing Limited.

Stevens, M. L. (2003) The normalisation of homeschooling in the USA. *Evaluation & Research in Education*, *17*, 2–3: 90–100.

Stevens, M. L. (2009) *Kingdom of children: Culture and controversy in the homeschooling movement.* Princeton, NJ: Princeton University Press.

Sutton, L. and Bogan, Y. (2005) School choice: The fiscal impact of home education in Florida. *AASA Journal of Scholarship & Practice*, *2*, 2: 5–9.

Taylor, V. (2005) Behind the trend: Increases in homeschooling among African American families. In Coper, B. S. (ed) *Home schooling in full view: A reader* (pp. 121–133). Greenwich, CT: Information Age Publishing.

Taylor, C. and Gutmann, A. (1992) *Multiculturalism and "The Politics of Recognition"*. Princeton, NJ: Princeton University Press.

United Nations (1989) *United Nations convention on the rights of the child.* Geneva: Office of the High Commissioner of Human Rights.

Van Pelt, D. (2003) *Home education in Canada: A report on the Pan-Canadian study on home education.* Canada: Canadian Centre for Home Education.

Vanderbeck, R. M. (2005) Anti-nomadism, institutions, and the geographies of childhood. *Environment and Planning D: Society and Space*, *23*, 1: 71–94.

Verger, A., Lubienski, C. and Steiner-Khamsi, G. (2016) The emergence and structuring of the global education industry: Towards an analytical framework. In Allan, J. and Artiles, A. (eds) *World yearbook of education* (pp. 3–24). New York, NY: Routledge.

Wacquant, L. (2010, June) Crafting the neoliberal state: Workfare, prisonfare, and social insecurity. *Sociological Forum*, *25*, 2: 197–220.

Webb, S. (2010) *Elective home education in the UK.* Stoke on Trent: Trentham.

Welner, K. and Welner, K. (1999) Contextualising homeschooling data: A response to ruder. *Educational Policy Analysis Archives*, 7: 13.

Wilkin, A., Derrington, C., White, R., Marton, K., Foster, B., Kinder, K. and Rutt, S. (2010) *Improving the outcomes for Gypsy, Roma and Traveller pupils: Final report, research report DFE-RR043.* London: Department for Education.

Wilkens, C. P., Wade, C. H., Sonnert, G. and Sadler, P. M. (2015) Are homeschoolers prepared for college calculus? *Journal of School Choice*, *9*, 1: 30–48.

Winstanley, C. (2013) Too cool for school? Gifted children and home schooling. *Theory and Research in Education*, *7*, 3: 347–362.

Yin, R (2003) *Case study research: Design and methods.* London: Sage.

Index

acculturation 103

A levels *see* examinations

Apple, M.W. 10, 13, 15, 25, 68, 122; and Redistribution of funding 29

autism 93–98

Badman Report *see* Badman Review

Badman Review 1, 12, 17, 19–20, 22, 118, 121

Bauman, Zygmunt 26, 33

Balls, Ed 20

Basham, P. 16–17

Beck, Ulrich 4, 9, 21, 22, 24–25, 25–28, 50, 82, 120; Cosmopolitanism 116–117; Individualisation 27–28, 103, 122; Negotiated family 122

Beveridge Report 12, 24

Bhopal, K. 2, 11–12, 18, 20, 26, 51, 53–54, 64, 68

Bourdieu, P. 35, 50, 119–120

British identity 103–104, 120

British values 118, 120–121

Castells, M. 116

Charter schools 10

Chief Inspector of Schools *see* OFSTED

Christian conservatism 14

citizenship 2

Cohen, Stan 22

Conroy, J.C. 30–31

cosmopolitanisation 116–117, 121

D'Arcy, K. 18, 51, 53–54, 64

Department for Education (UK) 1, 12, 84

Department for Education (US) 3

DfE *see* Department for Education (UK)

Dick, P.K. 119

disability 83–101

diversity 15–16

domesticity *see* intimacy

Douglas, M. 81, 118

dyslexia 86–93

Education Act, The 11–12, 20

Education Otherwise 12, 18

Equality Act, The 84

Esping-Andersen, G. 24

European Union 11–12

Evangelical Christians 14, 68, 111

Every Child Matters 19

examinations 34, 50n3, 57, 59, 73, 74

faith schools 31

Gaither, M. 16

GCSEs *see* examination

Giddens, A. 81

'gifted' *see* specialness

Gilroy, P. 103

globalisation 9, 21–33, 81–82, 116–117

gypsies and travellers 18–19, 26, 51–66, 120; gender roles 53; racism 54

Hall, Stuart 103

Holt, John 14

Home Education *see* Home Schooling and Home Education

Home Schooling and Home Education: Advocacy 27–28; Asia 12; Australia 12; Canada 10–11, 16–17; Europe 11–12; funding 29–30; gypsies and travellers 51–66; legislation 9–12; mass schooling 31–32; middle-class families 34–50, 119; regulation 9–12; religious families 67–82, 107, 111; South America 12; special educational needs 83–101; race and ethnicity 102–117; terminology 20n1; United Kingdom 11–12, 17–19; United States 3, 10, 13–16

132 *Index*

Home School Legal Defense Association 10, 14
HSLDA *see* Home School Legal Defense Association
Hysteresis effect 120–121

individualisation 27–31
intersectionality 21, 117
interest convergence 10
intimacy 32–33
Ishaq, Khyra 19
Islamisation *see* radicalisation

Kraftl, P. 18, 32–33, 100

libertarianism 14
localism 123
Lubienski, C. 29

Madrassa schools *see* Muslims
marketisation 119
Marshall, T.H. 2, 12, 24–25
Massive Online Open Access Courses *see* MOOCS
mass schooling 31
MOOCS 26
moral panic 22
Muslims 1–2, 74–80, 120; *madrassa* schools 81; Trojan Horse affair 81
Myers, M. 2, 11–12, 18, 20, 26, 51, 53–54, 57, 58, 64, 68

National Centre for Education Statistics 3, 15–16
National Curriculum 1
NCES *see* National Centre for Education Statistics
neo-liberalism 23, 27, 119
No Child Left Behind 1, 15

Office for Standards in Education *see* OFSTED
OFSTED 1, 12, 17, 22, 37, 50n1, 69, 75, 81, 87, 117, 118, 121
'other' 33

Passeron, J. 35, 50
Plymouth Brethren 68–74
Putnam, R.D. 58, 67, 80, 82

radicalisation 22, 117
Reay, Diane 2, 119
Ricoeur, P. 103
risk 1, 3–4, 9, 19–20, 22–28, 81–82, 103, 118–123; citizenship 23–25; disability 100
Risk Society 4, 21, 81–82
Rothermel, P. 13, 18
Rousseau, J-J. 29

SATS *see* Standardised Assessment Tests
Saturday schools 107–110, 115, 116, 123
School Attendance Order 12
SEN *see* Special Educational Needs
social capital 58, 67, 80, 82
Special Educational Needs 18, 83–101
'specialness' 83, 99–101
Standardised Assessment Tests 40, 50n2
'Stranger' 33

Trojan Horse affair *see* Muslims
Trump, Donald 122

United Nations 1
United Nations Convention on the Rights of the Child 2, 9, 84
unschooling 14

Wacquant, L. 23
welfare state 24, 31
Wildavsky, A. 81, 118
Wilshaw, Michael 1, 17